Borderli

A Me

edited by
Barbara Rehn

saturday night
Feb 4, 2012

There are 107,000 gay guys online at this very moment. But somehow, on a Saturday night, in one of the gayest cities in America, I can't get a single person to keep me company. Not even a single person to chat online with 'me. For the record: I would certainly date me, to be frank. I'm good looking, good in bed and good to people in general. But I know where my past has caught up to me, and I want to take this moment to bare my soul and let you, whom I don't even know, get a glimpse into my life and history and see why I'm now inside on a beautiful San Francisco Saturday night writing in my diary, struggling for any meaningful interaction with other people. I am going to quote a blog article that resonated with me.

"Being beautiful is a burden. People look at a beautiful person and have a wealth of stereotypes at their fingertips. Those who are beautiful try in vain to compensate for the connotations attached to their appearance. In the back of their heads, however, there is always one lingering thought, an oft-spoken phrase: you're nothing but a pretty face."
Thought Catalog. (2011, May 27) Eye Candy: The Burden of Beauty [Blog post].
Retrieved from http://thoughtcatalog.com/daphne-dcruz/2011/05/eye-candy-the-burden-of-beauty/

Beauty creates a strong sense of expectations – attractive people must live attractive lifestyles. But the pressure to constantly perform breaks us down much faster than the aging process. By my late teenage years, I was actively suicidal. I couldn't perform at the level that people expected of me based on my looks, and it took a strong emotional toll. Why didn't I have more friends? Why couldn't I be more active in the social circuit? Why wasn't I popular at school? Perhaps, in retrospect, I'm the only one that asked these questions, but they were relevant nonetheless. The more desperately I tried, the more miserably I failed. It was finally in my early 20s that an opportunity for a real breakthough came about. I was accepted on a full ride scholarship to law school in San Francisco (I lived in Seattle at the time), and I enthusiastically took the school up on that offer. While my undergraduate experience at the University of Washington had certainly been a step in the right direction, socially, nothing prepared me for the whirlwind of activity that was the San Francisco social scene. School, first of all and most importantly, carried the largest social burden, but as a gay male I also felt the need to represent myself in the Castro area. I have to say, I succeeded well, in all areas. I was elected by my entering class of roughly 250 students to represent them in the student body as a second year law student, to coordinate all their social activities. I had grand plans and the support to carry them out. Nothing stood in my way. Except one thing. I hadn't been in a serious relationship since age 16, if that one could even be considered serious, because of my abandonment issues. Abandonment = isolation = loneliness = ugly = worthless. Is that how the equation goes? I certainly had no doubt at the time. Nevertheless, I quite riskily embarked on a relationship with a boy around my age, mid twenties, in business school at the same university. We dated for perhaps three months. After that I left for a study abroad program sponsored by the school. We intended to maintain our relationship while I was temporarily abroad, but several weeks in, he called to break up with me while I was stranded in a foreign country. And I simply could not handle the stress. I immediately overdosed, was rushed to the ER, and then medically evacuated back to the US for further psychiatric evaluation. Over the following 24 months, I had no less than 14 additional overdose (OD) attempts. At first, they were related to this incident. Then, if I went out the bars and didn't get hit on "enough," I would go home and OD. The standard for what my life was worth dropped exponentially with each passing day, and my doctors were desperate for a solution. So desperate, in fact, that the State of California, on my 14th OD, refused to provide any additional care until I went back home to my parents in Seattle and completed mental health treatment there. When you've already been through the wringer, tried every medication and therapy approach there is to try, by age 26, you start to feel either that you're invincible for having survived it or that nothing really matters anymore anyways. So when I was offered drugs in exchange for sex, for the first time ever in my life (no, not even weed or cigarettes), I unhesitatingly jumped. Now, two years later, full-blown drug-induced psychosis having taken what was left of my sanity (at least temporarily), rehab having sent me back to the psychiatric ward and The City struggling to help me struggle to make ends meet, I sit at home alone on a Saturday night, wondering how to start over in the process of making friends and getting a new life.

beautiful mess
Feb 5, 2012

"A diplomat is a man who always remembers a woman's birthday but never remembers her age."
Robert Lee Frost (American Poet, 1874-1963)

Amen Mr. Frost. Ladies and gays, just like Peter Pan, stay young forever. At least, we admire youth forever. However, we get old, fat and ugly instead: Beauty is only skin deep. So, apparently, is the desire to be beautiful. No one wants to put up with the result, at least if they know what it entailed. On the other hand, everyone wants a piece of beauty. Muscled hunks? Yes, please. I just personally don't want to be wasting my life away at the gym every day. Blood, sweat and tears are not my style. I'm more of a chiffon cake kind of girl. Are we obsessed with beauty because most of us can't have it? If everyone was pretty, would we cease to care? If everyone was rich, would money matter anymore? The ripped muscle hunk isn't even a fair comparison, because he worked at his appearance. What about those born pretty? Johnny Depp and Orlando Bloom come to mind here. Or, for that matter, Robert Pattinson, as America apparently agrees with me here (according to People Magazine). When we are beautiful, there's always the temptation to wonder if we're beautiful "enough." When we're not, we'd take any part of being beautiful that we could have, screw the hierarchy of it! Is it because of People magazine that I intended to end my life over rejection issues? Is that any less ridiculous than blaming a bad night at the clubs? We've become so sensitized to what people think about us and our appearance that literally nothing else matters. On a typical night, I would go out dancing with 3-4 friends, have some cocktails, make out with a few random dudes and go home, maybe with one (or more) of them. But on a night when I didn't get hit on, or hit on "enough," those other times where I did have fun didn't matter. I wasn't beautiful enough right then and there to matter to these other people (complete strangers!), so life was not worth living. As soon as that thought would surface in my mind, there was no escape until I could finally get home and overdose. That was my only relief valve. In the gay community especially, perhaps, there is a great deal of attention focused on hooking up. If you go out dancing and don't go home with someone, you've let down the community. This creates a second set of unrealistic expectations: a) be beautiful, always, and b) hook up tonight, every time. The concept that I could even critically evaluate these statements and see how extreme they were didn't even cross my mind, and if it had I would have pushed it away. My reality was so real to me that it didn't matter whether it was right or not. My life literally depended on my version of reality, and it was killing me. So my ending thought/question/statement is this: if we pretend that age is "just a number," then can beauty be "just a number" too? Or does that only continue to perpetuate the fraud that we perpetrate on ourselves whenever we half-heartedly say and whole-heartedly do not believe that age is "just a number." We'll always notice beauty. What else should we be noticing?

beautiful meth
Feb 5, 2012

On the heels of my last post, "beautiful mess," I owe it to myself, my family, my friends and my readers to continue opening up about my life. If I were to be asked, right now, what was most important to me in life, what I held sacred or get most enjoyment out of, I would have an answer without hesitation: crystal meth. A beautiful mess. Crystal energizes me. It gives me purpose. It provides direction. It buffers me from the cares of the world. It makes the world seem OK again. It motivates me. It eases my pain. It enables me to be sexual. It lowers my inhibitions. When the world just doesn't seem to care, tweak is there. It's a lifestyle. What happens when you start to crash? Paranoia, delusions, exhaustion, emotional lability ... all things that can be avoided by simply taking another hit and keeping the run going. Why bother coming down? Staying up for two weeks at a time has become normal. Eating is a chore at best, voluntary masochism at the worst. The body simply does not want the food. Applesauce has, quite literally, saved my life, with crushed-up multivitamins mixed in to replenish my system. All pleasure aside, I remain addicted because the addiction fills a need. I must forget what has happened. I must recover and move on. My memories must be so covered up and cloudy that they cease to exist at all. If the good goes out with the bad, c'est la vie.

"I have absolutely no pleasure in the stimulants in which I sometimes so madly indulge. It has not been in the pursuit of pleasure that I have periled life and reputation and reason. It has been the desperate attempt to escape from torturing memories, from a sense of insupportable loneliness and a dread of some strange impending doom."
Edgar Allan Poe (American Writer, 1809-1849)

The question is not what I like about crystal. Rather, what has it done for me? It has broken up my relationships, caused me to lose my friendships, gotten me kicked out of my house, made me homeless, put me into the psych ward and forced me into rehab. Rehab ended six months ago. I remain legally "homeless," though housed in an SRO (city-run converted hotel rooms in old buildings), I remain on state disability and I remain addicted. Just one more hit. One more drug. One last time. Because tomorrow it will all be different. Tomorrow I will wake up and the world will make sense again. Tomorrow I will understand why I've been raped and abused, and I will accept that I can never be the same again. And tomorrow I will take back control of my life.

"I admire addicts. In a world where everybody is waiting for some blind, random disaster or some sudden disease, the addict has the comfort of knowing what will most likely wait for him down the road. He's taken some control over his ultimate fate, and his addiction keeps the cause of his death from being a total surprise."
Palahniuk, C. (2002, first pub. 2001) *Choke*. New York, NY: Anchor Books.

But for now, for tonight, tomorrow is so far off. I can keep my cloudy dreams, my tweaker body, my energy, ambition and lust for life ... and yes, of course, I can have another hit. Tomorrow never comes.

sleepless in san francisco
Feb 6, 2012

Restless, awake and discontented. Was "beautiful meth" the right approach to take? I've been judged harshly already on it for sharing my lifestyle so openly. There is definitely more to come about what my lifestyle actually is, but i think the real issue is my traditional insecurity around disagreement. My gut reaction is that I did something wrong. But in the process of growing, I need to stop and ask myself, "who are they to judge?" In this case it has been some of my friends, but the question still needs to be asked. More importantly, why do I care? I said what I needed to express, and people may think what they may. I still have my close friends, and most importantly I still have me. My life is on its way to becoming an open book. I'll have to learn to accept that some chapters may touch on topics that polite society doesn't address. Fuck politeness. I've nearly died keeping my story in. It must be told. If you can't handle the ride, get off the rollercoaster.

borderline affairs: a retrospective
Feb 7, 2012

Borderline Personality Disorder
-History of unstable relationships
-Past suicidal ideation and attempts
-Anger management issues
-Frequent rapid unpredictable mood swings
-Impulsive behaviors, including risky sex, substance abuse and recklessness
-Fluid identity
-Frantic efforts to avoid real or imagined abandonment
-Chronic emptiness.

PTSD
-Flashbacks to past abuse
-Avoidance of any reminders of the past
-Emotional numbness
-Difficulty remembering details of the abuse
-Prone to angry outbursts
-Easily startled

Depression
-Uncontrollable agitation
-Difficulty concentrating
-Chronic fatigue
-Feeling hopeless
-Feeling helpless
-Feeling worthless.
-Social withdrawal

American Psychiatric Association. (2013). *Diagnostic and Statistical Manual of Mental Disorders* (5th ed.). Washington, DC: Author.

I am all these things and more. Sometimes I wonder why. Why was I abused? Raped? Told I wasn't good enough? Why did it happen to me? Sometimes I wonder why. Why can't I pick myself back up and get going again? Why do others put their lives back in order but not me? Why can't I figure this out? Sometimes I wonder why. Why is therapy so difficult and protracted? Why, at age 28, do I take 9 different prescription medications a day for mental health? Why can't doctors just fix me? Sometimes I wonder why. Why do I so easily become addicted? Why have I thrown away a life on the right trajectory to become a homeless junkie? Why can I only feel all right when I'm high? Sometimes I wonder why. Why have the best doctors money can buy failed me? Why can't therapists just tell me what to do? Why can't social workers provide me some stability? Sometimes I wonder why. Why do I love somebody so easily? Why do I hate somebody so easily? Why are those often the same people, in a revolving crisis of emotions? Sometimes I wonder why. Why do my friends give up on me? Why does the world turn its back? Why am I alone when I'm the one that's been abandoned all too often in life? I can't answer these questions. Maybe I just don't care enough. Or maybe there are no answers. And so I continue to wonder.

suicide blonde

Feb 8, 2012

"Suicide blonde was the color of her hair / Like a cheap distraction for a new affair / She knew it would finish before it began / Woah baby, you lost the plan / You wanna make her, suicide blonde / Love devastation, suicide blonde / You wanna make her, suicide blonde / Love devastation, suicide blonde"

INXS. "Suicide Blonde." *X*. Warner/Chappoll Music, Inc., 1990.

I am suicide blonde. Devastated. Crushed. Hopeless. Faithless. Love passed by again. I can't keep trying. I can't fail anymore. When will I be the one that everyone wants? When will I have all the glory? Not yesterday. Not today. Tomorrow never comes. I went out to the clubs with a friend that fateful night. It was a balmy Saturday evening in San Francisco and all the boys were out in Castro. I ordered a vodka cranberry, as usual. I stepped on the dance floor, stripped off my shirt, and let myself free. It was a moment of liberation, of exhilaration. I stood out, but I fit in. I was one of the club kids, one of the regulars; this was my club. I ordered another vodka cranberry. Gave my bartender a kiss, as usual. My friend and I danced all night. The club closed. I was alone. Once popular on the dance floor, now solo in the streets. Waiting for my bus home. No one looked. I knew, right then, what had to happen. Sometimes people ask, what made you do it? Sometimes people ask, why? But they don't know, I was alone. Empty. Frightened. Angry. Confused. No one looked. I could have been anyone on that bus. Just another night. Drunk passengers. Uptight bus driver. Some of the regulars on the bus. Sporadically, a group would get on and off, clearly going to/from a party that I missed. I got off. Walked up my driveway. Turned the key. No one home. I live alone. I panic. Can I go through with this? I try and reach out. No one understands.

I reach for my pills. 20 sleeping pills. Counted and sorted. 30 anti-depressants. Counted and sorted. 20 anti-anxiety pills. Counted and sorted. I reach for a glass of water.

I called Mobile Crisis after the overdose. Police were sent immediately.

I had no choice. I couldn't run. I couldn't hide. The police were already there. Angrily asking me: what made you do it? Angrily asking me: why? I cried. I had no idea. Would I know before I died? A breathing tube down my throat. Charcoal to counteract the medication. Ambulance ride at full speed. But I don't remember this. Wake up. Wake up. Wake up. Four days have passed. I'm in the ICU with a catheter, breathing tube, IV lines creating trackmarks up and down my arms. What happened? I remember too well. Not the hospital. But that night. They medically clear me then transfer me directly to the inpatient psychiatric unit.

My psychiatrist arrived to take over my care. Another anti-psychotic. Another anti-depressant. More mood stabilizers. More anxiety meds. Different sleeping pills. The perfect recipe.

"Their tears are fillin' up their glasses / No expression, no expression / Hide my head I want to drown my sorrow / No tomorrow, no tomorrow / and I find it kind of funny / I find it kind of sad / The dreams in which I'm dyin' /Are the best I've ever had"
Tears for Fears. "Mad World." *The Hurting.* Phonogram/Mercury, 1983.

Rule the World
Feb 8, 2012

Saturday morning. 9 AM. Walking home from the bus, got off a few stops too early. Spent the night at a trick's house. Connected so well together, had the most amazing sex. Watched Beverly Hill Chihuahua afterwards. So cute. Got up at 7, made toast together and had some orange juice and coffee in his cramped kitchenette. Helped clean up the 300 sq ft studio with a view of the parking lot next door. Across the street was a male strip club. The walls were just thin enough to hear the traffic most of the night. The trick was about my age, shorter, brown hair, and an adorable face that to this day makes me smile to see. I'll never forget his name or our time together. I took the bus home in the morning and a song came on my iPod that I had never heard before. It soared and swayed, it tingled and teased, it literally moved me so much I had to get off the bus early to run down the street, arms wide open, singing the refrain at anyone I passed. This was life. This was worth it. I give this song to you because it saved me. It gave me hope and inspiration. It transformed a great night into a mind-blowing event, lifting me up, higher, higher, as I lay panting, gasping for air on my front steps, out of breath from singing in the rain. It has never failed to give me hope no matter what I'm going through. If it can do the same for even just one of you, I will have made my mark on the world.

"You light, the skies up above me / A star, so bright you blind me / Don't close your eyes / Don't fade away / Don't fade away "/Yeah you and me we can ride on a star / If you stay with me girl, we can rule the world / Yeah you and me we can light up the sky / If you stay by my side, we can rule the world

If walls, break down, I will come for you / If angels cry, oh I'll be there for you / You've saved my soul / Don't leave me now / Don't leave me now / Yeah you and me we can ride on a star /"If you stay with me girl, we can rule the world / Yeah you and me we can light up the sky / If you stay by my side, we can rule the world

All the stars are coming out tonight / They're lighting up the sky tonight / For you / For you / All the stars are coming out tonight / They're lighting up the sky tonight / For you / For you, / Yeah you and me we can ride on a star / If you stay with me girl, we can rule the world / Yeah you and me we can light up the sky / If you stay by my side, we can rule the world

All the stars are coming out tonight / They're lighting up the sky tonight / For you / For you / All the stars are coming out tonight / They're lighting up the sky tonight / For you / For you"
Take That. "Rule the World." *Beautiful World (Import).* Polydor UK, 2006.

cracked

Feb 9, 2012

I know what you're thinking. "If you didn't do drugs, your life wouldn't be such a mess." "You can't escape facing your fears forever by getting high." "It's the drugs that ruined your life, that made you try to kill yourself." I know what you're thinking. And maybe in part you're right. Getting high did make me go crazy. Getting high did help me escape my reality, stop me from facing my fears. Getting high did make me suicidal. But that's where you're wrong. Out of fifteen suicide attempts, one – ONE – was by drug overdose. Until 15 months ago, I didn't even know what drugs were, beyond some vague idea that "drugs were bad". I knew that I'd tried everything else. Psychiatric medication since age 16. First psychiatric hospitalization at age 19, voluntary. My psychiatrist said I could start taking 800mg/day of Seroquel per a new research study. Or take an MAOI inhibitor. In other words, every medication and combination available to modern-day psychiatry had been tried and discarded. I could try theoretical doses of powerful anti-psychotics, but no one knew if it worked outside of rats, or I could take first-generation anti-depressants that largely don't work at all, at least not without significant side effects. And I tried talk therapy. Of course, it seemed like a joke most of the time. Some of the best psychiatrists in the nation couldn't even diagnose me, let alone treat me. So go "talk" about it ...? Well, I tried. To this day I'll never know if it didn't work because I just didn't try hard enough, or if it didn't work because there was no way it could have worked.

First psychiatric hospitalization at age 26, involuntary. Medication overdose. Second psychiatric hospitalization, age 26, involuntary. Medication overdose.............Fourteenth psychiatric hospitalization, age 26, involuntary. Medication overdose. Transferred care back to Seattle; California Department of Health refused to treat me further until I stabilized at my parents' house.

"Wanna party?" I was online looking for guys. Sure, whatever party meant. I love parties. I asked. It meant "tina." I knew that was a drug but wasn't sure which one. Thought about the proposition for a second. I was at the laundromat using the web browser on my cell phone. I had moved out of my parent's house back in with my old roommate in Seattle. We lived on a boat. There were no laundry facilities there. It was a sunny day. Blue skies, no clouds, just the type of day that tricks a tourist into thinking Seattle has beautiful weather year-round. It only took a second. Why not? What did I have left to lose? What did I have left to try? Anyways, it was just sex. The drugs were incidental.

I learned a lot that night. About love, and lust, and desire. I learned a lot that night. I learned I could never have sober sex again. I learned a lot that night. I learned that I could be happy. Not just content, not just seeing past the pain, but actually Happy. No one had ever told me that this was what it was like for everyone else to live life. I realized I had never genuinely smiled before in my life because there was no smile in my heart. But now .... now I knew. And because I knew, I no longer had to die.

"I'm safe / Up high / Nothing can touch me"
Pink. "Sober." *Funhouse.* La Face, 2008.

I've remained out of the psychiatric ward since that first hit. They want to make me go to rehab. I say … Just one more hit. One more time. Death is calling.

RIP Amy Winehouse.

please don't go

Feb 10, 2012

"Love is a dirty trick played on us to achieve the continuation of the species."
William Somerset Markham (Novelist, 1874-1965)

My mistake, in retrospect, was that I needed it more than I wanted it. I needed to be in love, needed to be loved. But its true: you can't love someone else until you love yourself. I didn't even know myself, let alone love myself. I needed my partner to not only love me, but literally to complete me, to define me. He had to love me enough for the both of us. It didn't work. How could it have? Its been ten months since we broke up. Well, we'd been broken up but I couldn't accept that, so I kept hanging on for months after it was over. After all, we lived together, how could we be separated? And besides, I loved him, wasn't that good enough? I thought being a little puppy dog, following him everywhere, giving him cute sad eyes, constantly begging for attention, was love. I thought putting up with fighting, screaming, violence, was love. I thought, why I am not good enough for him? What was he searching for that I couldn't provide? [Aside from mental stability, financial stability, ability to take on responsibilities around the house, etc.] But I couldn't do those things. I was too busy scrambling to fix the loss of love. There was nothing more important in the world than that I regained that love. Wait ... no. What I mean to say is, until I regained someone who could love me enough for the both of us. I didn't know that at the time. I just knew I was failing.

"I really need you / Just like the air I need to breathe / I'll stand beside you / I'll never leave / Don't go / Don't go"
No Mercy. "Please Don't Go." *No Mercy.* Arista, 1996.

Kicked out to the curb. Just like happened to me earlier in life. How appropriate that it was precisely ten years later. Nothing like a decade gone by to reflect and reminisce on the past ... or relive it in excruciating detail. What did I learn about love? That I'm not good at it? What does loving myself mean? How can I measure and graph and chart that, with an absolute start and end point? And isn't there a shortcut somewhere, somehow? I learned I love too easily. I learned I reach for the nearest person to complete me. To define me. To accept me. To love me for the both of us.

"Reach out and touch faith / Your own Personal Jesus / Someone to hear your prayers / Someone who cares / Your own Personal Jesus / Someone to hear your prayers Someone who's there"
Depeche Mode. "Personal Jesus." *Personal Jesus (Single).* Sire/London/Rhino, 1989.

aloneness

Feb 12, 2012

a lone ness (n.): (1) a state of being alone, isolated or insulated, even though surrounded by and being interactive with others (2) seeing oneself as if in third person, being one step removed from one's social environment, observing oneself interact with others seemingly without active participation in the moment

"I walk a lonely road / The only one that I have ever known / Don't know where it goes / But it's home to me and I walk alone / I walk this empty street / On the Boulevard of Broken Dreams / When the city sleeps / And I'm the only one and I walk alone" Green Day. "Boulevard of Broken Dreams." *Boulevard of Broken Dreams (Single).* Reprise, 2004.

I had friends. I had lots of friends. In fact, I was elected by 200 of my peers to be their class representative for our class' second year of law school. I was constantly holding parties and events, or heading out to the clubs, or studying in study groups or just grabbing coffee with friends. I was social, at least by law school standards. But I was empty. Driven forward by some external force, but I wasn't in the driver's seat. All I could do was observe life happening to me. I remember the moment so clearly. I'd just been released from the hospital after a 5-day stay in the psychiatric ward. As always, I was there on a "5150" – California's legal code for "involuntary hospitalization – harm to self or others." I don't know how long I'd been at the main hospital before being released to the psychiatric ward. I'm not even sure what I overdosed on. It was 9:00 am. I was wearing the clothes I'd been brought in with, vomit stains on the pants and shirt. My face was cut and scarred from my valiant attempt at shaving with the hospital-issued single-blade razor (under the supervision of two nurses, of course). My laces weren't put back into my shoes yet; they had had to be taken out as a safety protocol. I had tape from IV lines all up and down my arms and some bruising. I still wore my ID bracelet, as if the plastic bracelet was the closest thing to jewelry I'd seen for a while. My school was a 20 minute walk from the hospital. I knew I could just make my class. And I did. I walked in late. The room is set up lecture hall style, with the lecturer at the podium front and center and bleacher-style seating, accommodating 100+ people per class. I came in through the front door. No one even looked. I took my seat. My friend had made a copy of her notes for me from the classes I'd missed. She didn't ask where I'd been. It's the problem of "the boy who cried wolf." I wasn't threatening to take my life – I was actually going through with it. But it didn't work so many times that people started to view it as a simple threat, not as a call for help or plea for intervention. And they stopped asking where I'd been while I was absent from class. I never told them I was in the psychiatric ward. I had simply said "hospital." The first few times, people cared. After a while, they stopped coming around. I was in and out of school so sporadically that I lost contact with most of my friends. Is it strange to leave the psych ward and go directly to class? Is it strange that people just don't ask? Funny that I went from aloneness to being alone. Surrounded, but not engaged. Popular, but unaware. Sex and rock-n-roll, life in the fast lane, but it wasn't me driving. And then, death. But it wasn't me dying.

"can't you see, it's not me you're dying for? / now she's feeling more alone than she ever has before / she's a brick and I'm drowning slowly / off the coast and I'm headed nowhere / she's a brick and I'm drowning slowly"

Ben Folds Five. "Brick." *Whatever and Ever Amen.* 550 Music/Caroline, 1997.

wonder
Feb 12, 2012

i sit, my legs pleasantly crossed, my tie tucked in, my briefcase at my side
i wait, my mind focused on the tasks ahead
i wonder, where is my ride?
i wonder, did life pass me by?
i confess, i've always wanted this to end
i pray, take me from this earth
i pray, let this time be the last time
i pray, give me an ending, save me from my life
but i discover i can't die
i resurrect
death refuses to take me yet
i return to where it all began
i wonder, where is my ride?
i wonder, did life pass me by?

rape me, my friend

Feb 13, 2012

I first had sex when I was 16. It was with my boyfriend at the time, also 16. We were on my co-worker's houseboat. She had lent it out to us so my boyfriend and I could lose our virginity together. She was an amazing resource. My family disapproved (to put it mildly) of sexual relations, but my co-worker was a professional dominatrix (as a side job). She taught me how to put on condoms with just my mouth and a flip of the tongue. She taught me when to use condoms. I "accidentally" used her handcuffs one day when she was gone and she had to come back and rescue us since she had the only key. I learned a lot from her.

I first got raped when I was 16. It was with my boyfriend's pseudo-adoptive step father. Essentially, a guy who had taken him in. He was about 45 at the time, freelancer and professional photographer. That's how he got the boys. We all needed photos for our website profiles, and he offered beautiful photography for free. I met my boyfriend through him. It was an odd triad. I could only see his "son" if I would have sex with the father. Turns out that was on an ongoing basis, as if my time with my boyfriend needed to be renewed with every act of sex. There was no pleasure, no joy in that sex. Just duty and pain. I didn't know that other people didn't have to sleep with the father to get the son. My parents never told me.

"Rape me / Rape me my friend / Rape me / Rape me again / I'm not the only one / I'm not the only one / I'm not the only one / I'm not the only one / Hate me / Do it and do it again / Waste me / Rape me my friend"
Nirvana. "Rape Me." *In Utero.* Geffen Records, 1993.

I first started experiencing sexual difficulties at age 21. Not the Viagra kind of difficulty. The kind, rather, where you're not sure if sex is ever appropriate because it is an act of essential domination and humiliation, in which only savages could participate. This was alternated by periods of extreme lust and sexual abandonment, all risks explored. Then swinging back. Someone must be the object in sex. It is an object-subject relationship. The subject penetrates, the object gets penetrated. It is passive, acquiescent, submissive. I couldn't handle being any of those things. So I wouldn't pursue sex or dating. It wasn't until age 28, after trying to block my memories with every imaginable technique – therapy, medication, drugs, alcohol – that I finally realized why I had control issues. Its all obvious here, but the revelation was incredible. I'd been fucked up for 12 years largely because I'd been fucked by the wrong person. I'm angry. 12 years of my life spent spinning in circles because I couldn't complete school or hold down a meaningful job while I had to worry about others telling me what to do. At the same time, I was completely helpless. I couldn't even pick out a brand of ice cream at the store by myself. I put others in the awkward position of having to help me, knowing that I would hate them for helping me, and sabotage them if they didn't help me. But I didn't know this was all related. No one ever told me. So, today, I know. I'm learning how to pick out ice cream at the store. I'm learning how to stand up and say no. I'm learning that others aren't always right, especially when it comes to how I use my body. But this all takes time. In the meantime, I sit and wait. And I wonder. Did life pass me by?

desire in his eyes
Feb 14, 2012

fuck me harder
give it to me

i look away in my mind
still there in the bed

who am i?
whatever he wants
whatever he desires
i'm someone though
i matter to him, right now i matter

i look back
still fucking?

refocus

it hurts

refocus

i can't let him know i'm in pain
i need to be whatever he desires
otherwise who am i?

i look away

in my mind he loves me, he wants me, he desires me, we're happy together

i look back
done
i'm numb
"thanks sexy"
pack up and go

refocus

there is no love
nothing but momentary desire
and for just a moment there
i felt alive

my secret garden
Feb 15, 2012

night falls
my time to shine
rays too feeble to be seen
against the harsh light of day
but oh how glorious
against the darkened sky
my hours
once and forever
protect me, insulate me
isolate me
but never abandon me

i slowly rise
my glow emanating forth
my pride, my glory, my sanity all there all safe
just not in the day
not yet
not ever

my secret garden

morning breaks

Feb 16, 2012

abused i run
let me break free
break away

i have my friends to protect me, encourage me
late at night we play
we chat
they lift me up
they keep me company
remind me that there is hope

morning breaks
i need to go back
slowly i walk around the corner back to my house
explain where i've been

"kirk, there was no one out there
just you,
alone
curled up in the dirt"

thorazine dreams
Feb 16, 2012

all the lights are off
it's cold inside
the power has been cut off
roommate is gone, off to work
i'm left here

its dark
its lonely
its agonizing
its irresistable

had i just had a bad day? week? or was it just that i could do it now?
the pills were all too accessible
lithium, thorazine, trazodone, ambien, risperidone, clonazepam
i knew it was a toxic combination
i knew i wouldn't feel a thing

so i did it
for whatever reason
or none at all
i just wanted to
why not
what's left to lose?

counted and sorted the pills, 20 of each, very precise
laid down, my mattress on the floor
i was moving out of the house soon
everything else packed up, broken down
just like me

i shivered and trembled in the cold darkness
alone

and i dreamt my thorazine dreams
fuzzy and sticky and sweet
calm and peaceful and encouraging
whispering to me: "everything will work out now
this time
just rest, don't fight it"

why do we do this?
Feb 21, 2012

why do i do this?
why do i do this?
make believe that sex is love
make believe that sex is more than a temporary connection
make believe that i like this person so much
despite the abuse

it starts simply enough desire, passion, shared between us
i can see it in his eyes, in my quickening pulse
it's just a fuck

but i see it as more
i see it as love
as validation
as encouragement
as if being desired somehow transformed me and my life
into a life worth living

i play my appointed role
pretending to be ready for anything the night brings
but i'm not
i must be whatever he wants
otherwise, i'm not desirable any longer
i'm trash, thrown to the curb
i'm empty, gone with the wind
i must remain desirable

i tense
it hurts
but i can't say that

it's done
i run to the restroom
i need a moment
to cry
to numb the pain
to pretend it didn't happen

it's over and desire is gone
he got what he wanted
did i?

desirability
i had it for a second
but the pain, the agony, the tears

yes, i got what i wanted, for that one brief second
and then i got what i deserved

planned homelessness

Feb 25, 2012

It's a bit strange. Planning for homeless. A bit like planning for an abortion, the loss of your loved one. By the end of this week, I have to leave my current residence, despite my doctors, my case workers, the City itself, all knowing that I have no other legitimate options. Suddenly, when their resources run out, I'm just a stranger to them too. So I plan, alone.

Too sick this week to even get out of bed. Swollen neck, itchy scalp, body rash, high 10-hr fevers. Next available appointment at the public health clinic? 2 weeks. I take it. I have a plan. I've got a few, actually. Nothing that will support me for long, but hey, I never wanted to live long anyways. Start escorting? Start dealing? Bring it on. So I'll have a place eventually, guaranteed. The guarantee is "eventually." Maybe they'll give it to whatever children my family manages to produce.

The City says "move along." The City says "we couldn't help." The City says "its not our fault our programs failed you." When the program fails, blame the victim. Must be in their administrative manual. So, sure, I've got a life full of opportunities ahead. Hope, though? What have I learned that should keep me hopeful? No, I think I'll give those opportunities to others who will use them. I don't have much else to offer to give away before I die.

rain falls

Feb 26, 2012

i walk forth, my world crashing and falling all around me
if you listen just right, its like a gentle rain whispering to me in soft tones of hope and
inspiration
the rain picks up
all the opera seats are full the patrons leen in, frowning
what will he do with his life now?
will he recover and get a job and find his life again?

the rain turns torrential now
the gentle rain, the gentle hope, washed away
will he listen to the torrential rain, and give up hope, as should have been done long
ago?
surrender to the sweet mercy of drug-induced happiness, where the rain never comes
and the music never stops?

but i can't decide today
i don't ever want to decide

the rain will never stop pouring until i've made up my mind
until then, the rain falls
just life restoring death

well-watcher
Feb 27, 2012

men desire me
my coy dimpled smile

men desire me
my natural blonde hair and blue eyes

men desire me
my fitted tee's and tight pants

men desire me
shirtless

men desire me
not ripped, not cut, not slim, but lean

men desire me
cause i got moves like no other

men desire me
with a tip of the hat,
dancing on the dance floor transitions to dancing in the dark

men desire me
the heat, the passion, the intensity rising

men desire me
cause i'm sexy and i know it

why does desire feel so sorrowful?
like watching a well fill, so many words, so many phrases, cast in
yet the well remains, just like the words,
empty

dissociative violence
Feb 28, 2012

what i wanted was to be held, to be told everything is ok,
to be told i'm loved
what i wanted was a bond of affection, a meaningful touch,
a lasting connection

but men are primal, lusting after one thing only
don't tease
don't shake the cage
i am only as good as the tricks i can perform

i need to disassociate
i need to break away
the violence is coming, i know it
why have i done this again to myself?

because i wanted that momentary affection
i just hoped that this time, it might last

we pass a few hits back and forth
he gets horny
i get mellow
detached
distant
uninvolved
like the violence is happening outside of me

and we fuck
and i'm good
as long as i can see his desire, i can keep going
but i don't want this
it hurts

i can feel the pain slowly breaking past the drugs and infiltrating my consciousness
"another hit, please?"
how long can i keep up this charade? how long 'til the drugs don't work anymore?
if i force myself to find seeming pleasure in the violence, am i respecting myself?
am i a proud icon of the gay community?
or am i just a common whore?

when I leave, do i hold my head high walking down the street, having just made my conquest?
or do i try to hide, having failed myself yet again?
all i know for sure is that i satisfied him
maybe i can push away the pain and tears and be satisfied at his pleasure
after all,
its all about the desire in his eyes

dog days

Feb 28, 2012

When the dog days come to tear you down
When savage beasts are stealing your crown
When wild and crazy just don't seem like fun anymore
When they find your bruised body, washed up on the shore

Remember
You're not alone, little one
You're a survivor, my precious son
Beyond the roaring wild pack the sun still rises in the east
And one day, you too, can join this opulent feast

Carry on, tiger of the dark
The path to go is less than the path you've come so far

We make you take this journey so you know that you are strong
So you can look back and say, I was never wrong

Remember
An unexamined life is not a life worth living
But a man who ascends from the ashes, that is a life worth giving
Keep on, little tiger of the dark
Your day is dawning, hear the angels hark

unanswered

Mar 3, 2012

> "Exchange ourselves / And we do it all the time /"Why do we do that? / Why do I do
> that? / Why do I do that?"
> Pink. "Fuckin' Perfect." *Fuckin' Perfect (Single)*. La Face, 2010.

why is it like this?
things all the same
don't people say that things always change?

why is it like this?
trembling in bed
don't people say that love heals, not hurts instead?

why is it like this?
voices in my head
don't people say your mind's only quiet when you're dead?

why is it like this?
the agony, the pain
don't people say life gets better every day?

why do i go on? when going on is so, so wrong
why am i like this?
i know i'm not that strong

personal jesus

Mar 4, 2012

i am destined to walk a long, winding road
full of hardships and the unknown
but yet, despite all the pain and tears i shed
there he is, my own personal jesus

no longer walking alone down this path
no longer failing to find the words at this task
i am lifted, higher, to dizzying new heights
my own personal jesus came through, tonight

i soar high, above the rain
lifting me up, out of the pain
i see the promised land ahead
my own personal jesus, saved me from the dead

its not too late
to change my fate
i am strong enough to survive
this, my own personal jesus already realized

hand in hand
we walk the sand
life makes sense
my own personal jesus tears down the fence the fence that divides my right mind from
insanity
the fence that was built up, by me
the fence that saved me all these years
can go, now that my own personal jesus is here

who is this man that i adore?
no partner, no spirit, no conquistador
my own friend, my own love, my own happy land
my personal jesus reaches out his hand
and two become one
am i the father or the son?

i am my own personal jesus
i can save myself, no need for blessings from above

preview: gunplay
Mar 7, 2012

A man
With a gun
Pointed at my head, pistol barrel ready to be spun
But hell no I don't play that game
I know the streets, I've made some fame
I slept with his son
Made peace with my past
Then the jilted lover comes out to kick ass

The father, drunk and violent now
Pulled a gun on me, hoping I'd cow
I kept my level, I stared him in the eye
"I know why you're here, but I'm not going to die"

I'd slept with the son, but not with the father
He'd raped me already, why should I bother?

And so, with a silent exchange
He lurched by in his drunken way
I let myself in the house
Laid down on the couch
And pondered
And wondered
Where is the end of this mental joust?

gunplay
Mar 8, 2012

We parked the car ("Mother Mary full of grace, help me find a parking space"). It was my coworker and I from the restaurant; everyone knew we had a crush on each other. We were headed, after a busy day at work, to my brother's studio to relax for a few hours until he got off work too. A man was at the front gate. He was engaged in conversation with two teenage skateboard punks. They looked frightened and yet amused, as if the conversation was barely making logical sense. When Orlando and I (names have been changed to protect the innocent) arrived, the man turned around, sensing that there was new company. The teens ran inside and stood watching and waiting from the inner glass doorway. They wanted a show, they just didn't want to be the actors, apparently.

It took me a full minute, at least, to recognize the man. He reeked of alcohol, clearly just released from the drunk tank down the street. He appeared still intoxicated, stumbling over himself and his words. I don't remember his exact words, but whatever he was saying, it was directed at me, personally. Something about fucking around with the wrong people. That's when I finally knew.

You see, a few days before, I had flown back into town from San Francisco. On a free day, I contacted my ex, my first boyfriend, and made plans to hang out at his place. Yes, this is the same ex that had the molesting father. But I figured my ex was (somewhat) innocent in the whole plan, and I looked forward to seeing him. He was in a relationship, fairly serious, at this point, but we fooled around anyways. I left, comforted by seeing him and yet comforted by knowing for sure that I no longer found him desirable. A phase of life I could write off. Or so I thought.

It was Scott at the door (names have not been changed since there are no innocent parties here). My ex's father. The had-been rapist. The former photographer for my nude pictures. And the current drunk standing in front of me. My mind raced. He must have been told by his son, my ex, that I was back in town. Being a resourceful man, Scott must have looked up my brother's address, or I had given it to my ex and he passed it along. I'm still not sure how he knew to find me there, and how long he'd been plotting and waiting to carry this out, but no matter what, this was not an accidental meeting.

The gun came out. His other hand was gesticulating wildly about whatever he was saying. But the gun hand was steady, held straight at me, point-blank range. My friend was clearly desperate to leave, but all I could focus on now was keeping us alive.

I have no idea how the conversation went. I know I was confident in my interaction, even telling him to put down the gun and leave, that his son and I were finished, etc. I remained very calm under pressure. In case you haven't guessed, Scott wasn't necessarily upset that I saw his son. He was upset that I didn't see him too. Like it had become a mandatory part of our protocol that I had sex with the father whenever I had sex with the son. "Scott, go home. I can't help you. I can't do what you're asking." Both our words droned on and on, but the gun stayed right on target. Leave it to the teenagers inside, watching, to not call the police to handle the situation. Were they expecting a video-game style shootout? Except only one of us had the gun? Reminds me of the scene from Chicago, "and we both reached for the gun!" One gun, two people. Who wins? I wasn't about to be bullied. Not that day. And not in front of my friend. So I kept my cool. Told him he was drunk, he needed to rest and sober up, then we could discuss. Eventually, finally, after about 15 minutes (or was it 5 that seemed to drag on?), he gave up, put the weapon away, and walked off with a big "fuck you." Fine, I can handle that. But not literally. And that's where, for the first time, I drew a line between myself and an "other," not letting them define me and tell me what I can and can't do with my body. That night, on my own, maybe for bravado effect for my friend, maybe just because I finally had the confidence, I stood up for myself. And I won. It took a long time after for me to stand up for myself again, but I at least knew that I could do it, even under extreme circumstances.

I never saw Scott again. Or my ex.

today, i can
Mar 11, 2012

one day i hope to comprehend it all
make sense of it all
find meaning in it all

one day i hope to find true love
to discover real happiness
to connect with another

one day i hope i can forget it all
put the past behind
live for the tomorrows, not the yesterdays

today, i can move forward with my life
hold my head high
knowing i'm ok in every way

Faster
Mar 14, 2012

So we walk faster
Trying to escape our past
Striving to drown out our history, our pain
Afraid that we can never be free

Moving on, pushing ahead, leaping forward
All these terms
I'm not the only one wanting to break free

But where are our gods? Our idols? Who has overcome?
Our past shadows us, like a dark demon, waiting to be let out

I don't know that I'll ever be free
These fallen angels, they follow me
Every step is quicksand
Every "go" pushing back
But I walk faster
Trying to escape my past
It must not last

Stop
Mar 16, 2012

"Stop"
I can't
I can't say it
Not like I mean it
Jokingly, perhaps
Or subtle signs
No one catches on
The act continues

Who am I to say stop?
Who am I to deserve respect?
Why stop now?
Why here?
So I continue
Defeated
At my own hand

Why do others always assume?
Why is the assumption always yes?
I try harder
To assert
To demand
To simply ask
"May I excuse this round?"

I can't say it
I don't believe it
Such a simple word
Such a bewildering world

What I say
Is what I say
I simply mean
"Stop"

crying
Mar 25, 2012

i force my eyes open
devoid of sleep
yet not ready to let the world in

i am surrounded by my failures
defeated even by my triumphs
few as they may be

life is too harsh
too real
too literal
too fantastical
too much too much

i try and remind myself of swinging in the park
of sunny days and laughter
of hearing dogs bark
memories all gone
faded
never to be lived again
if they were ever lived at all

i can't open up
i can't let people see
head held high, heart held low
i want to reach out and touch someone
know that what i see is real
yet scared of the reality of what i see

i can't take it
i can't make it
i give in and give up and give over myself
to another universe
to another world of possibilities
to another life
anything but this

i cry out, silently screaming
hoping for a helping hand
knowing its already too late
i'm dead already, even before i have died
nothing left to give
nothing left to get

nothing left at all
just a hollowed out shell of a former man who once believed he had it all

sometimes
dying is a way of crying

<u>fucking</u>
Apr 29, 2012

Sex
A dirty word
Yet often used so lovingly

I say fuck
Straight to the point
No hidden agenda
No feelings
But all the glory

I say lust
I mean desire
I mean the undeniable temptation to rip off a stranger's clothes and fuck senselessly and endlessly
I know who's in charge here
Take me as I am
Make me do things no other man can
And always begging for more

Sex
An act of domination
Of brutal violence, of men raped and left for dead
A tool of destruction
Ruining friends, ruining partners, ruining lives
A double-edged sword leaving no parties uninjured

I say fuck
Because proper language cannot describe the feeling one should have but lacks when being intimate
Is intimacy a form of power too? Can we separate domination from sex, intimacy and fucking?
Is intimacy dead? Nothing more than a mere physical connection on a random night with a stranger in bed?
Is this what I've aspired to?
I never wanted a wedding
But love and companionship, I thought I could find

I leave it to historians to debate when sex became just another mindless fuck
Who gives a fuck
About me

I say fuck
What do you say?

inspiration
May 1, 2012

my mind goes blank
stutter
recall
no recall
no movement
no life
no inspiration
yet

do i go on? like this? who am i? where am i? who are you? how did i end up here? and,
one thing makes the world go round but another makes it good
do i like you? do you have what it takes?
to be a man? to be a person? to be a human? to be my superhero?
my life, my movement, my terrain, my everything
wrapped up, balled up, crying, screaming
who am i? where am i? and,

life is precious
life is pointless
use it, abuse it, wear it out
there's only one, or is there?
i should know, i must know
i feel the sensation, the emotion, the river of tears, crying, screaming
"why me?"

life is precious
life is pointless

on the suicide bed
May 13, 2012

no one can know
these things i think
these moments i endure
no one can imagine the depths of my disgust
with myself

failure is the only thing i've got
succeeding at losing keeps me sane
now they want to take that from me?

i look up into a blank room
walls, ceiling, floor... all empty
except a solitary mattress on the floor
i'm agitated but excited
no one around
no one to know
ignorance is bliss, they say

i've tried too hard
i've fought a losing battle
i am unworthy .... yet unrepentant
giving up is all i've got left
this bag of tricks has run dry
am i unloved or am i unlovable?
i know the answer
i feel it every day

i was cursed with life, and i am taking back that power
only i control my destiny
the remedy is in my hands
i've tried it your way, you hypocrites and whores
seducing me and abusing me
no more

tonight, i finally feel
alive

Flip

May 15, 2012

Life
And death
Flip a coin
Woightod, ploaoc
I may not know the outcome
But fate is on my side

If I commit the act, the consequences must follow
Yet, they don't
I live on
Defying hell
Resisting the news of my resuscitation
Who dared to interfere in my own plan?
Who sought to leave me helpless and hopeless?

The coin flipped
I call heads
And before it could finish, I finish myself

Heads, indeed
Take mine, here, for posterity
I love you and I hate you
You did this to me

Saved me? From misery?
Well guess where I'm headed back to now
Save me now, you bitches
Except you're gone
Crisis is over
Or has it just begun?

hopeless romantic
May 24, 2012

I should be with someone
I should complete another's life
I should be happy
Or at least content
"Should's" are all I know
Insufficient is all I am

I was raised to believe in the sanctity of marriage
Of one man and one woman
Of heaven and hell
And of a brutal God

Today, I've found my own way
Life is not straight and narrow
Life can never be lived that way
Am I a sinner? Am I in hell?
I know the answer, because I believe in me
Someone, somewhere must complete me
And I must complete them
Til then I live my life among prostitutes and whores
Learning the beauty of the Underworld and all she has to offer
Learning to be addicted
To lust, to life, to love
High off the energy she brings, high off the substances that have given me new life,
high off the delirium of a crazed man in a crazy world, I find my own place
A place just for me

Heaven and Hell can drag me down
But I know my own truth
I am complete
I have found me
Amidst the rubble and the ruins, the needles and the pipes
I've seen the hypocrisy of marriage, the tragedy of life
I may be a prostitute
I may be a whore
But while you fester in your rotting marriage, I let myself be
I complete me

No more "Should's," no more ultimatums, that's a game I've quit
You had me in my childhood, taught me right and wrong, good and bad, and how to
pass judgment on others different from I
I couldn't
Perhaps they weren't different

Perhaps I was them, in a different or future life
Underneath my plain khaki pants, my button down shirt, my neatly combed hair, I knew
I didn't feel right, I simply felt compelled by those who came before
By those who never questioned
By those so eager to find someone to complete them, they rely in blind faith on Jesus
and in God
As if alliance with the deities is an absolution of what has before transpired, the
wickedness, the hatred and the condemnation
No, those actions are inescapable
And judgment will come

You may call me a prostitute, you may call me a whore
And you'd be right
But I love myself
And have found those who love me

The hopeless romantic finds love in all the strangest situations
Why not find love in yourself?
Why not find love in anyone you choose?
Ignore the condemnation, we love you for finding your own self and support you for
showing who you are
"You're beautiful"
I'm a hopeless romantic for beauty

Once more, with emphasis
May 24, 2012

What is it about her?
My association runs deep
It used to be a choice
Now it's a lifestyle
Handed to me on a silver platter
With a spoon of stone weighing me down
But I hold on
"Never let go," she whispers "I can make you all right"
And I believed
I had nothing else
Lines on the mirror
Rocks in the bowl
"Just one hit," she says, "just one more time"
And I had it all
And I lost it all
Nothing but smoke and mirrors and hazy memories of a life once lived
Surrounded by dismal ruins and decay
Evidence of fun once had, of tears once cried, of lovers and of friends
All gone

I don't want your rehab, your morals and your cures
I want her back
This time for good
I long for her embrace, soothing and safe
Up high, nothing can touch me
The world around me crumbles and dies
And I sit back, numb and emotionless
I don't want to feel
Take away the pain
I never let go of her
My spoon of stone
My rock of solace
The hand that feeds is the hand that binds

Just one more hit
And everything will be all right

Mirror

May 25, 2012

I put down the crack pipe
Look in the mirror
I see
A vacant mask staring back at me
But not my face, no
Surely I would know
This mask staring back is not at all what I meant to be

I've had good fortunes
And I've had bad
Time takes it toll, this I understand
But this doesn't look like a man
My reflection mocks me

Staring into space I reach out to grab it, to throw the mask out
So I can see the real me
I cut myself on the sharp mirror glass
I feel the blood dripping down my arms
Horrified, i look in the mirror
Nothing but a vacant mask staring back at me

Choice
May 30, 2012

I've had many choices in life
Many opportunities to reflect
I've had the privilege of learning new things and meeting new people
When we make the wrong choices, pain and suffering follow
I was raised to believe there was only one right way, and defiance or ignorance was a morally reprehensible choice
I was taught to believe that people choose actions that maximize their self interest
I was taught to believe that guns and wars were necessary to keep our chosen way of life protected
I was brainwashed to believe that certain choices bring moral condemnation
I was shown how poor choices were dealt with, behind closed doors
I know life is what we choose to make of it
But I never chose to be gay

prisoner
Jun 3, 2012

I can't take it anymore
This constant persecution
This extraordinary bondage
These chains of steel, weighing me down

I am assaulted
By venomous lies about me, my person, my manhood
By embarrassing truths that should not see the light of day
By ragged distortions of my past and present self

I am chained down
Struggling to survive
Hoping and trying to make my way out of this dungeon
To someday see the light of day
But I am held down
Warned to stay back
Told that seeing the sun is not my proper role in life

I am a shadow dweller
My perseverance only weakens me
My fight for truth and justice is lost in the stupefying silence
My only hope for survival
Is to stand in the shadows
Content with drippings from the plate
Satisfied with insults and contempt

My dungeon master spits daily in my face
He shows me the unworthy beast that I am
He tells me to give up the fight, give up the hope, there is no tomorrow
He tells me to fall back on my sword for my missteps
He tells me to give in, to accept the punishment, to acknowledge my sin
He tells me who I am and who I'm supposed to be
He tells me

He is me

White-washed

Jun 6, 2012

Sitting in the corner
Face down, between my legs
Looking at the blank, white wall
In a white-washed world, there could be an entirely new existence
One filled with exuberance and hope
But not tonight
The footsteps behind me indicate he is coming again
Not satisfied with anything but total possession of my body for his use and pleasure
The bootsteps come closer
I look to my wall
Can't we all just be whitewashed away?

As the abuse occurs, I never stop believing
In that white, blank slate of a world
Pain and agony wrack my body
Pushed in positions I didn't even know
Made to do things that dogs won't even do
Humiliated, abused, chained and miserable
Did he win?
Did he finally possess me so much even my emotions are his?
I must remember
Those white-washed walls, they speak to me
There is an alternative, they say, to all the beatings and abuse
You just have to find your own way there
So I did
In a bottle of pills
On a quiet wintry night
My corner defied me, mocking my efforts to join in
All I had to do was grab on
But I was grabbed away

Forlorn now, sure to be forgotten
"Is he another suicide prevented?"
You tell me
I begged heaven and hell to take me away
To that land of white-washed walls
And I almost made it

Once again I sit in the corner
Looking at the beauty of simplicity, the elegance of nothing
Admiring the plain white walls
And I hear bootsteps behind

This time I get the punishment of a runaway slave, harshness to match my coldness in escape
How much longer can I hold out hope?
I must get to the white-washed land
I see it every day
I alone have the bridge to the other side
If only I don't get caught
I could be as happy as a lark floating free in the wind
Or could continue this path of horrors and despair

Both feet on the ledge now, I wait til my accuser is near
So I can spit in his face
Then jump as only the desperate can do
I am no longer in control, spiraling downwards
All I know is life couldn't get any worse
And maybe, just maybe, I'll crash into this white-washed world

live strong
Jun 7, 2012

Restless
Discontented
My mind races
My heart, even faster
I lie awake at night, thinking
What have I done? and
Where did I go wrong?
Believe me, I am strong

But strong enough to stare temptation in the face?
Strong enough to hold jealousy and rage at bay?
Strong enough to hide my inadequacies so that none could see?
Strong enough to refuse that first, merciful hit when offered to me?

I am not
Not that strong
Recovering from my failures and my haunted past
Moving forward despite the injury and pain
Looking upwards when all I want to do is drown
This strength saves me from putting myself down

I don't understand most of what goes on
Let alone what has transpired
My mind, in a continual fog
Reaching out to activate arms and legs as if motor controlled
With plenty of equipment malfunctions
I forget routines and daily tasks
I forget that special promise I made to you
I forget what the conversation is about, before it ends
This fog must go, but I'm not strong enough to push it away
Nothing can clear it and show the shining day

Except when I'm asleep
Dreaming beautiful dreams of a life that could have been
Desiring the world but woefully unprepared
Itching to prove my worth
Instead, falling on my sword
Intent to do it right, this time
Only this time never comes
Last chance for the prom night dance
And I'm home, alone

What else have I messed up?
Please tell me somewhere I've done good
Because I'm restless to show the world
But too often leave my flag furled
Nothing more than a passing mistake,
A blink of an eye
I'm gone
Or does my damage live on?
I must stay strong

Future tripping
Jun 10, 2012

Desperate for answers
Looking for some guidance
The future remains out of touch

How am I supposed to move on
When failure is the only game I've got?
The demons of my past
Torment me
Make me repeat my mistakes
Only to fail to learn again

Fuck that
I've been through hell and I'm not going back

The future is unknown
One day at a time is all I can take
I'd peer into my crystal ball
If I thought it contained any answers
But fortunes are won and lost only on the battlefield
I can't stay low forever
I must get back into the game
Past be cursed and future unknown,
All I can do is make the present my own

Clawing out of my hole
Reaching up, up towards the sun
I deserve the right to be happy, demons be damned
There's still so far to go
But look how far I've come
I never thought I'd escape my low

Press on
The demons of my past can stay in my past
I'll take my chances on a new life
I foresee pain, loss and suffering
But also compassion and caring and joy
Learning to live in a fucked up world
Learning its ok to not hate everything
Learning there are some moments actually joyous
And learning joy can be felt no matter what the state of the world

Learning to live again
One step at a time
But each step further from the past than the last
Until the future becomes known to me
And I can break the bonds of my past

Turning point

Jun 17, 2012

I sit alone
In solitude
In a prison of my own design

Where are the friends that I once had?
Those criminals, so righteous, so bad?
Why do I sit here now, so sad?

I wonder where this trajectory began
At what point was I irreversibly destined to end up like this?
Was it one year ago, when my relationship ended?
Was it two years ago, when my addiction began?
Was it there years ago, when I was on a suicide spree?
Was it four years ago, when I entered law school?
Or was it in my childhood, some mistakes that I made, perhaps
Or some wrong I had done
Or my penalty for being gay?

My mind wanders
Tripping over the tiniest of stones
Which stone was it that sank my ship?

I can't recall the turning point
Perhaps things just randomly happened
Or perhaps I don't care to recall

All I know is..
Here I sit
In solitude
Wondering what happened to my life

Yesterday
Jun 24, 2012

Yesterday, I cried
Where can I find myself?
I seem to have lost my way

This barren jungle assaults me
Temptation at every turn
But no forgiveness, no, not today

I search my pockets
I search my soul
Is it too much to ask for a little light this way?

Do I find me in the smoke filled rooms at night
Come morning, fade to black
Is this my future, never seeing the day?

Do I find me in the cloisters and circles of privileged lives, of lives unburdened by the weight of the real world?
After what I've been through, I don't fit in
There must be a safer place, some way

Yesterday I cried
I lost my self, my dignity, my life
What will the day bring, today?

Alone

Jun 28, 2012

Alone
I am
Cut off from all worldly pleasures
Living in pain

I reach for my nirvana
In a bottle of pills
Take away this damned day, week, month, year

I want to pretend it never happened
I want to feel numb
I want to display my hurt to the world

In pills lies salvation
Overdose, my aim

Pull the blankets tighter
I have no shame

Before I slip away
I feel
Alive
The joys of life become clear
I understand so much

Then it melts away
Into
A vast sea of darkness
Where I am
Alone

Sinking

Jul 14, 2012

Sinking slowly
Drifting by
Where have the hours and the days gone?
Vanished
Up in smoke

I cry out
But no one seems to care
The burden of my weight
Too much to bear

Once lonely days and lonely nights
Now filled with the wild excitement
Of people who don't care
Smoke being the only enticement

Do I continue down this path?
Can I even turn back?
The life is sucked right out of me
The will to carry on
Is gone

Who now to save me from drowning?
Who now to bear that giant cross?
Who now to hold my hand?
Who now to give a damn?

Lonely days and lonely nights
Surrounded by the revelers
But seeing through the party
What is there?

Time
Feb 24, 2013

What happens when time runs out?
When the sand falls through the hourglass no more
When all our cares, our fears, are gone
When the hopeless can finally rest in peace

When time runs out I plan to be
Naked and carefree, running down the beach
Chasing kites, chasing dogs
Chasing me

I've spent my life in vain
Trying to find me
To figure out who I am
To know the unknowable
To console the inconsolable
To finally make everything alright

When time runs out I plan to be
Steadfast, yet heartbroken
Waltzing to a different beat
Stumbling on truths, like crocodiles in a marsh
Chasing forever after
Chasing me

Time has ended
I am the killer of time
The taker of lives
The undertaker of destiny
The destroyer of dreams, of fantasies, of visions of life
Was any of it real?

Time has ended
But who am I to know
What have I taken?
What has been lost?
I've gained enlightenment, truth and peace
An inner calm in an outer death
Dreams may be destroyed
But only if the dream is to not be destroyed
I live on, like the grains of sand in an hourglass
Turn me over, right me up, let's go down the rabbit hole again

Untitled

Feb 28, 2013

> "At least the addict fixes the time, place and manner of his own death"
> Palahniuk, C. (2002, first pub. 2001) *Choke*. New York, NY: Anchor Books.

This is wrenching to read but easy to relate to. Just seeing the flame made my heart surge in anticipation of a literary shot in the arm. How many suicide attempts I made is uncountable, how many lives I destroyed is unfathomable and where my life has ended up is unthinkable. Drugs kill. But oh they feel so good. Would I trade my future for a hit? What have I got left to trade?

<u>Fuck you</u>
May 6, 2013

To all my critics in the methadone clinic
To all the crack whores littering my streets
To all the trannies working my corner
To all the nay sayers gettin' detoxed in it

Fuck you

I can do this on my own
I dont need your help, your lies, your support
I may be down and out
But I ain't desperate for that flailing line

...of coke, cut out on the mirror in front of me
Neatly packed lines, fat and heavy

No I don't need that flailing line

....of ecstasy and crystal
Ready for a treat, holding steady

No I don't need that kind of flailing line

"Here honey, have a drink
It kills the pain
Until you too are ready"

No I don't need that kind of flailing line

Crystal kills. It numbs the pain. Who cares what happens to me in this fucked up world,
long as I got my baggie and a pipe. I can make it on my own.

Until I die.

Don't give in, that battle is not yours to win
Don't let up, temptation all around
Don't lose sight of the goal, of happiness, of truth
No more hiding in the shadows
This bird wants to break free

I may have to save myself
The critics, the liars, the thieves .... they don't got your back
Your friends, your heroes, the ones you call late at night .... they ain't there 'cept if you
need some crack

But I want to be there, even if I'm alone, waving my little flag
For justice, for peace, for me
No more whack

No one turns down a line
But they can turn down a friend
No one refuses the next hit
But they could escape the seedy hotel
Get on, I say, git

Maybe I'm ready, maybe I'm not
But when failure stops being an option, its time to start living again
I noticed the sun today
I grinned

Missing

Feb 28, 2013

Like a thief in the dark
You took my heart
Just for fun
And now I'm done

But look at what you left behind
Just like Columbine
Shrapnel strewed across the floor
Now who you calling "whore?"

I never want to see you again
But wait, I love you, don't ever let this end
Can I ever be of just one mind?
I tell my friends, "I'm doing fine"

My heart beats on
Though you are gone
What did I miss?
Besides your kiss

I love you, I hate you, don't leave me no more
Tearing lives apart, walk out the door
I never should have let you in
But that's how things begin

Out of my life, out of my mind
Creeping up when I say I'm doing fine
Like a shadow in the dark of night
You were never really gone

Reach for the stars
May 23, 2013

It was the best of times, that worst of times
Make my reality disappear
I find the horror
In every situation
I find the truth
Beneath every lie

Celebrating life
By dying
Celebrate success
By refusing to take part
There is no light at the end of the tunnel
There is no way out

So silence your gods, your priests, your shaman
My reality, they cannot touch

Here I am, all alone
Find me, kiss me, make me your own

Fuck that
No one cares
My tragedy, they laugh at me
My reality, I disown

There is no truth
Only the judgments of others
On which we choose to rely

I want my life back, the one I never lived
I want my freedom, far from sin
I want to reach for the stars
Falling short
I fall back

This existentialism, it betrays me
This religion, it disowns me
But this reality, it embraces me
Its' cold comfort all I've ever known

And all I'm meant to ever know

This thing we call life
Are we really living?
This thing we call death
Are we really ever free?
From the cares and the burdens
And the wasteland behind us (surrounds us)

Reach for the stars, they say

I fell

If that was heaven
Where is hell?

Chastened, I stumble
Whipped, I crawl
This reality is killing me
This life is bringing me down

Until my only feeling
Is sweet misery
The bitter taste of irony
The bucket full of blood

Reach for the stars, they say

I fell

Crucifixion
May 29, 2013

I am me
The undead
I see what others can't
I hear things others do not hear
I feel things others cannot feel

I have been saved, forgiven, restored
I have been wept over, agonized over and angered
I was not yet dead
But I had taken the poison pill
Let nature run her course

Intervention
Ending up in strange places and cold environments
Despising those who brought me to life
When all I wanted was the comforting grip of eternal peace

A piece of me is sad, a piece of me is glad
No matter, I must move on
Battles up ahead, rejection to face, tears to uncry
And bodies left to undie

I am the undead
I see pain, hunger and strife
I hear wailing, cries and agony
I feel coldness, emptiness, loss of sanity
But I do not feel alive

I have risen
I have come back to life
But looking around, is this a life worth living?
Should I renew my efforts?
Or slowly fade away?

Having been snagged away from heaven
Life on earth is a living hell
So we cope the best we can
And supplicate our hands
If I fade away, can I please be forgotten?
Can my tombstone say that I found life elsewhere?
Can my eulogy say that I won my death?

I am the undead
Living in the midst of you
Yet not of this earth
Oh sweet death, I'm ready for you, come take me away
Where life has happier days
And the undead shall torment the earth no more

Waiting

Jun 8, 2013

Waiting for a lover that never cares
Waiting for a lover that isn't there

She stands by the ocean, kicking some rocks
He stands by the ocean, learning the docks
Worlds apart but bound together
An invisible thread that connects us all
But the faster they come together
The harder they fall

He comes to meet her
She opens her arms
Dizzying possibilities
For a girl from the farm

Each moment that passes
Is a moment that lasts
Each kiss they exchange
Beneath the pouring rain
Means she has been found

He pulls away, but he is too late
Destiny has already sealed his fate
She, his lover, forevermore
He, defeated, kicked to the floor

Fuck that
Oppressed, he runs
Just a little girl from the countryside
With such hope inside her eyes
With such burning in her heart
She's come a long way from the start

But she'll never be like the others
Falling in love underneath the covers

His love was fleeting, ephemeral at best
Her love was strong, laying oceans at rest
She was hurt, again, by that great feeling
She held her head down, now kneeling
Before the altar of life's pleasantries
Here she makes her enemies

Too weak to go out alone
Too lost to go on her own
She screams at the rivers and the trees
"Why me?"

They mock her, their eternal presence
Her life, measured in mere seconds
Of flashes of love
Of rivers of life
Passing by

She cried

Waiting for a lover that never cares
Waiting for a lover that isn't there

Valentine's day memo to my ex

Feb 9, 2014

What of us?
Together, forever

What of us?
Dancing in the rain

What of us?
Movies under blankets

What of us?
Strolling down the beach

It's over now
That love long lost
But forever remaining in my heart

"If only"
"What if"
Should I have done something different?
Something better?
Something I've never had to do before?

"Us" held together
"Us" held strong
In the moments of breakdown,
"Us" was there
Staring long into the mirror

He wasn't perfect
But he was mine
A fortress against a dark, dark world
A respite from the tidal waves of life
A man to call - "my own"

Its been a year now
Looking back
I see the good, the bad, the fun, the sad
His family at a picnic
His friends at the bar
His life, intermingled with mine
Just waiting for the day
Waiting for the moment
When it's all fine

And still I wait
Some things I will never know
Why did he leave?
What sorrow did he know?
What sordid life he must have faced
As he lay there in the bed, all alone

I couldn't be there for him
I tried all night and day
I gave my all to save him
I used my strength to try -
And I failed
And I fell
And I cried

Nothing can save him now
Nothing can wake him now
As he lays in the bed, all alone
Life pulsing in his veins
Life pulsing through his bed
Life pulsing....

Life is short
Too short, some say
I don't know if what they say is true
Life is perfect, in every way
Every day
Life belongs to us
We take in and breathe out
A rhythm to the night
A whisper in the day
A pulse beating our way

...

And when life is gone
When life moves on
Take solace in the memories
Take comfort in the songs
Know passion, know truth
Know that your love was strong

...

He lays in the bed all alone
He lays in the bed -

Dead

In memory of Chris
Dedicated to his loving parents, Alan and Hilda

You don't know love until it's gone
And then you know,
It's not just a song
It's not just a lyric, scrawled on paper
It's not just a heart, carved into wood
It makes you live, it helps you try
Even
Even....

In those moments when we die

I love you Chris
I always will
May heaven treat you well

Pretend
Feb 19, 2014

Make believe that I'm all right
Make believe that morning is better than night
Make believe that I've battled and won the fight
Make believe that I see the coming light
It's all pretend
These feelings
I'm all alone

Who now to carry my cross but I?
Who now to suffer up on high?

And higher

Nailed up but floating away
Crown of thorns worn all day

Martyrdom is a curse

Give up these things
Or give in
Worship the higher power, the higher truth
The high life
The sin

Clouds roll back to reveal the day
I see it now
Sunshine gleaming off the dust in the air
The morning dew lightly touching the flowers so fair
And I..

I cannot take it
I run the other way

That life is not for me
I exit, take a bow
And run breathless to my maker

No, not maker
Not of original sin
But the maker within
Revitalizing, cherishing, giving strength
All I must do is give thanks

By going higher
Far above these worldly things
By tasting clouds
Out of reach of what the nighttime brings

I've given myself, completely
There Is no turning back
A martyr for the desolate
A citizen of truth
I alone carry the cross that I must bear
On the mountain, up high

Make believe that I'm different, changed, reformed
Make believe that inside I'm not torn
Make believe that darkness is not the shield that I've worn
Make believe that higher I go no more

It's all pretend
I'm all alone
Up high, so low
May my maker make it so

Darkness
Feb 19, 2014

Alone in the darkness
Feeling the chill as the cold air seeps through the windowpane
I've thrown myself against the wall
Into the corner I fall

"Whose idea of heaven is this?" said the cynic to the warden
What of heaven? Yes, I've given up long ago
Cold, frigid nights in the cellar are all I know

But with fire in my lungs
Breathing in, sipping down, drinking this sweet elixir
All my pain is vanished
Yet, my name, tarnished

So sit back and judge
"He did it to himself, really."
At first I did it to get high
Now I do it merely to get by

I've claimed my misery in that sordid prison of my mind
I've welcomed the warmth of the fire against the cold, dark night
Finding refuge in the one thing that I know
Here I am, just digging my own hole
Alone, now, at last
The party is over, the fun is done
What was once a ballroom dance floor
Has turned into simply wanting more

A shame, a life so wasted, so young
But who will ever know?
Alone, in the corner sit I
Alone, in the corner, getting high

Rise

Feb 22, 2014

Morning sunshine
The warmth embraces me
Surrounds me
Everything is ok

Look at my lover
Lying in bed next to me
So supple is he
I want you more

The daylight beckons
We come running forth
Let the day run its course
We're together now

A full day, a beautiful day
Spent together with you
Looking forward to you
Bless us today

Life is precious
Too full to experience alone
I could never make it on my own
Sweet lover, stay by my side

For what is love
But not the blossoming forth
Of life running it's course
May every moment be spent with you

Memories of our youth
Pouring forth into our future
Let life be our teacher
I love you

Nothing so certain as your rock by my side
Nothing so sweet as the love that we feel
Nothing so sacred as the kiss with which we seal
Our love, our bond, our eternity

Step forth into the daylight
Where the sun beckons and shines
Where I can make you mine
And share my life with you

Sweet forever, take us today
Sweet eternity, take us away

Pain of perfection
Mar 3, 2014

When life gets you down, it's so easy
To look at millions of people, just like me
Living in a universe where nothing exists
Living in a time where nothing subsists

Materials cast away, long ago rotten
Memories fade away, long ago forgotten
Families end
Relationships crash and burn
And so I turn
To the one true god I know to exist

Injection
The pain of perfection
Life oozing through my veins
Heart pounding to keep me sane

Memories forgotten? No, abandoned
In favor of a higher truth
Materials cast out, friendships lost
In favor of preserving our youth
Forever young, forever yours, forever speaking truth

I hold in my hands the power to change the world
But who wants that when I can change me?
I am hurled
Down into an abyss
Where lives have been lost looking for bliss
The pain of perfection, indeed
Man so fragile when in need

I can't change
World, beware
The temptress is here
To gather your young, the innocent, the free
To show them the sun, the life, the eternal seas
Worlds collide, but we don't care
All we need is here and near

Temptation indeed
Offering a life that is carefree
Promising a path of lightness and glee
With no turning back

To face the act
Of that first choice, to consider
Whether the pain of perfection is all we should live for
Or whether we whither
Away

I can't say
I know where I stand
With my fellow man,
Me
Taking my hand
Walking in the sand
To an eternity of bliss
That is what I live for

Let the clouds roll away
It's time to face the day
Nothing subsists
But in this, I exist

Welcome to my eternity

Clown
Feb 6, 2014

I'm fighting every day to become a better me
It takes strength to go on
But I see what I want to be

Not some junkie, found in a ditch
Some addict that OD'd... What a pity they say
No, I ain't that kind of bitch

I've hustled, yeah
Taken care of my own
When the stakes are down and out, and you're all alone
There ain't no time to moan

Suicide
So powerful
Gripping, tantalizing, mesmerizing
But so illusional, like a shimmering oasis in the desert
So undeniable...

So refutable.

I ain't no common whore
Never even saw the trannies on the floor
Stepping out into the sunshine, I wince
And wonder

Who have I been all these years?
Who's the stoic that never shed a tear?
Where's the man that brought me down?
It is I, like a fucking clown

Shamefaced
But oh, not me
Looking forward into eternity
I've lived my life, I've had my past
But no regrets for who I've been

I just, one day, look forward to being a better version of myself

Sweet nothingness

Mar 9, 2014

No one told me life would be so rough
No one warned me that tough isn't tough enough
No one cried for me when I shed my first tear
No one comforted me when I crashed down the stairs

The staircase we call life, forever spiraling upwards
Or is it downwards?
Does it know no end?
Only when we fall and it fails to catch us round the bend

No one told me life would be unfair
That some are happy, some are sad, some destined for love, others destined to die
It all seemed glorious, miraculous when I first started
Like life being lived up high

But then I fell
Into my own personal hell
With no one to tell

Crying only makes the pain stronger
Defeat is its only goal
So I humble myself before the box of pills
With the power to take away all my ills
And all my cares and concerns

"Just take them all at once," they whispered
I obliged, and felt my spirits start to quiver
If this is life, I want to live forever
This sweet nothingness, take me away
I've suffered long enough, my friends
Come now, take me, make this my end

A blissful scent, a beautiful sound, a tunnel into eternity
No past life flashed before me, just future yet to be lived
Cares and concerns replaced with hopes and prosperity
And sunshine as far as the eye could see

No one ever told me heaven wasn't real
That my entrance had been denied
Crashing down to those who "saved" me, those who brought me back to life
Did anyone ask if I wanted to die?

I've done my best to quit this game
If trying ever counts
Heaven stolen away, this lonely earth all that's left
No one ever told me I was born to be sad, but destined to never die
Let the demons win, I give in!

End this agony we call life
Stop the ride throughout the night
Subdue the creatures in the dawn
So I may go on
Unbothered, unintimidated, all alone, weary as a stone, simply subsisting

This is the life I was given
There is no light at the end of the ride
I'm left to to die a sweet death that never comes
Because no one ever told me that pain cannot be undone

alice falls
Mar 17, 2014

pop more pills
feel the chill
live the rush
die
just a crush

an addiction, all my own; a lifestyle, one i chose
may i get another?
life, i mean
this one doesn't go down easy

a flicker, flame, beacon in the dark
a spoon, a pipe, doing it on a lark
who hurts when i fall?
not i
not i at all

a bottle in front of me
a decision to be made
do i take the medicine?
or swallow the poison pill?
isn't that really what i've been doing all along?

alice
see through the looking glass
can you still fit through that door?
has life become just a chore?
drink the potion, my sweet
lie down beneath these sheets
when it's over it'll all be over
when it's done your time has come

hanging on, not letting go
i want to feel the thrill
again
of life
beyond the pipe

i want to feel the rush
of waking, flush
with life

it cuts like a knife

slit your wrists
smoke a bowl
live or die, who's to care?
who's to hurt?
not you, not i

alice fits through the door again
i am ready to embrace this sin
falling out, falling in
sodomy between me
and my pipe
outrage
pathetic

poetic

like a pill about to crush
like the damned who live for the rush
i take my pills
and live the thrill

and
i die
alone
needle in my arm
pills strewn around
who's to care? who's to know?
i just wanted to go
through the looking glass, again

Promises
Apr 19, 2014

I need you, don't hurt me
Please take all my pain away
Help me feel what it feels like to fall into an embrace
Show me a kiss that doesn't end with a serpent's tongue

Too long I've been searching
Climbing up mountains
Swimming upstream
Afraid of every bend, terrified of every slope

I've been hit on by stones, beaten like batter
I've been crying in my corner just to ease the pain away
Small respite it provides me, small companionship it holds
From the terrors of the world, those I know

Promises, promises
Like the changing of the guard
This time, you see, really, things have changed
I mean, why not try?
Just another sojourn through hell

Dreams are what you make of them
Stories to be told, lives to unfold
Or the great gnashing of teeth of a serpent, down by your feet
Insidious in its torment, ceaseless in memory

Yes, now I know, the serpent can be crushed
My life taken often enough
The blood of my forebears, the taste of my flesh
Time to quell the dragon, time to end the pain

Time to discover life anew
Full of promise and hope
Gone are hatred and suffering
Gone are the serpents at my feet

Promises, promises
And I promise you this
Every mountain, every stream, every stone
Is not for aught, is not in vain

Indeed, my dreams may stay
They were part of what made me today
A child, yes, tossed about in his crib
But now a grown man, and forever I can -

Make the most of lives untold
Slay serpents in my sleep
Wake refreshed with every new day
Raise the battle cry of life worth living

I promise you this

Upward bound
Jun 23, 2014

There's a funny thing about being homeless. After enough time, you start to accept that this is a legitimate way of life, that this is how things always have been and always will be. It's depressing on the one hand, liberating on the other. No longer bound by the rules and structures of society, I am free to pursue my own dreams and passions. Except, just a few years ago, my dream and passion was to become an IP attorney with my own secretary, a condo downtown and a great boyfriend. Today, I'm pretty thrilled when I get something hot to eat. That's almost more of an accomplishment than my prior dream - scrapping by on the streets takes a special courage and a certain fortitude that anyone who has not experienced such a loss could never understand. It's a daily battle, walking through alleys strewn with sharp needles, spending nights vigilant over what possessions you can still claim, and trying to make peace with your fellow men who are, as you, an outcast, an abomination, a failure.

I never chose to be this way. Six years ago, I had a complete mental breakdown. I not only was suicidal for a year following, but repeatedly attempted to take my own life. Life was hell, being ravaged by apparitions and voices and deep, dark depression. Suicide? That was my outlet, my escape valve, my reset button. It gave me a sense of serenity, knowing that I still held ultimate control, the ability to determine whether I lived or died.

A year of suicidality finally came to an end. I was healed, in the same way that a soldier is healed - patch up all the wounds, cauterize a few emotions, and send him back out to the battlefield. Or maybe more like Frankenstein - bits and pieces of different pills cobbled together in some makeshift fashion, the end goal simply being to stop the creature from taking itself apart. Rehabilitation? Giving life? These concerns were hardly even secondary; as far as I could tell, they didn't exist.

So I was forced to drop out of law school, despite a stellar reputation, good grades and scholarships, because I was a liability to the University. Having a student commit suicide while enrolled would certainly not look good in the US News and World Reports rankings. But kicking him out to fend for himself? That statistic doesn't show up anywhere, except to the detriment of the student who now has to explain why he dropped out of school.

Well, trust me, there was a lot of explaining to do. How does a bright, successful and privileged person end up living in a hospital, falling out of school, and giving up on life? How did it happen literally overnight? I didn't even realize there was a problem until I broke. So, no, I don't have answers to these questions. I can explain what happened, but can never explain "why." I needed that to be sufficient, enabling me, like the ex-con, to somehow regain a foothold in life. I tried to go back to my old career. I didn't realize how broken I was. You don't explain a year of hospitalization. You can't explain your sudden, public meltdowns. You can't explain the gripping anxiety that prevents you from leaving the house. You can't explain seeing people that don't exist, voices that never spoke, and events that never transpired. You just can't explain.

So I drifted from one job to another, moving from full time with responsibilities, to part time with few responsibilities, to "whenever I could make it out of bed" with no responsibilities whatsoever (and commensurate pay). I suppose my boss was doing me a favor, keeping me employed despite my obvious shortcomings. But really it just delayed the inevitable. I was no longer the type of person that could hold a job, that could be held responsible, that could live up to expectations, that could function in normal society. That person ended the moment I broke down so many years ago, it just took me this long to realize I couldn't make it any further.

I did my stint in drug rehab, like every other schizophrenic who's used drugs to calm their world. It only made me more suicidal, as they took away my medication without replacing them. After a few weeks unmedicated, I was a broken mess; my peers were frightened by my violent outbursts mixed with inconsolable crying, and the staff was frightened by me throwing chairs and stones and lamps at whoever dared to approach or touch me.

Finally, a break occurred.

It's funny how, when you land at the bottom of society, you find so many others just like you. They existed on the same street corners I used to walk by. They lived in the same hotels, shelters and cardboard boxes that I always hurriedly walked past. They were artists and actors and other professionals who had been brought down by life, cast aside by society, and who had created an other-world within, but separate and invisible from, the rest of the world. For the first time, I blossomed. I learned how to survive on the streets, I picked up artistry and acting skills from artists and performers, I worked hard to keep my head above water, but above all, I found fun. I found fun in my peers, my friends and companions, who stayed up with me at night, who jumped the turnstiles with me to go on an urban adventure, who created art so beautiful it made me cry. These people were not slogging through a 9-5 job, they were living an enchanted existence, a life where they loved what they did, where they were proud of their accomplishments, no matter how great or small, and where they relished what each new day would bring. These were not the failures of whom I had always been warned, these were real people living real lives with real passions and real dreams and aspirations.

Funny how my only aspiration is to just survive another day. Actually, that's not true. My dream is to make a mark in this world, to show others that those in my condition are not failures and rejects, to display to those who knew and cared about me in my past life that I was a survivor, and to prove to the world that my peers and I were not trash on the street corners, not failures at life, not incompetent or handicapped persons, but people who have learned that life is meant to be lived. I may never drive a Porsche. I may never see inside a Hilton. I may never become a lawyer, with my own secretary and a corner office, but fuck... I'm a survivor. I braved the worst of life and came through with my head held high. I learned about beauty in the smallest places, in the most inconsequential things. I learned that I don't need fancy things to make my life worth living. I'll still try and climb to the top, but I'll never regret this experience, never see homelessness the same way, and never just walk by a person on the sidewalk thinking I'm too good to even smile and nod. When you pray to your God, don't pray that people like me get risen out of poverty; pray, instead, that you may learn to love and care for those less fortunate, pray for compassion and understanding, and give thanks to those who, in some small way, have made your world more beautiful.

Funny how things change. Funny how they've never changed at all. Shift your perspective and you'll see, I've been right beside you this whole time.

The choice to choose

Jul 12, 2014

Life is full of choices. Life, itself, is a choice. We are born unwillingly into a world in which we know nothing, but of which we are supposed to partake and in which we are supposed to interact. None of this is a choice, until we rise up against the system. We can choose our selves, our identities, our values, our goals, everything that makes us who we are. We can choose everything that makes this forced life become a life of choice. The act of choosing, of comparing and selecting, of contrasting conflicting values, this is the heart of life. Without conflict, we are reduced to simply "being." "Being" has no life, no love, no soul. If we want to reclaim our souls, we must choose conflict, we must choose choice. There is no wrong choice, so long as the choice is freely made. Let the only unwilling act we ever commit be that of birth. Beyond, we have a responsibility to break free of the bondage in which we arrived. This is an awesome responsibility. Humanity advances at your discretion. It advances at all our discretion. What values do we choose? What morals will we believe? What kind of life can we build that makes that life a life worth living? We have broken free from bondage; cherish the choice we have been given.

Today, I chose life.

Yesterday, I didn't. Every day is a renewal of choice, a renewal of faith, a renewal of love for ourselves and others. Yesterday, I couldn't renew. I didn't see the point of going on. I didn't see the awesome power of choice. Because behind all our choices is the essential, ultimate choice: the choice to go on, to live on, to grow and spread and make this life your life. But I stumbled over the essence of choice. I chose not to go on.

Today, I was saved from the cruel hand of my last breath. Choice, again, taken from me. The choice to even choose the choice to live, that essential choice had been denied. There is no other. We must then go on, and on and on, knowing there is no other way. When the bottom of choice falls out, the universe is revealed as clockwork. But no, not that clean. A battlefield, rather, where each actor thinks he asserts his own destiny, and must do battle against the thinking-unthinking others. A milieu awaits, the skies go dark, the universe is broken, for choice is no more. Predestined to end that way, I suppose.

So, today I chose life.

Memories (a love affair)

Jul 22, 2014

I fell in love, with him
A partner
A comrade
A saving grace
A helping hand
A boyfriend, mine alone

Who knew, it would end so soon

Dinners every night
Breakfast in bed
At work, it was thoughts of him in my head
Loving the one who loved me
For the person that I was

And I was
Addicted
To him

Moving in, so it begins
A place in his bed
A spot to rest my head
A man who cared, who dared to love
A broken boy like me

I needed him, much more than one ever should
I needed the food, the room, the bed
I needed the good, the kindness, the roses all red
I needed to share the night
I needed to share myself
I needed his love
A love that stabbed like a knife
I thought love was supposed to hurt

Because love
Because there is no other word
Because love
Was a thing I never felt, not to myself
His love was all I knew
His comforting arms, his warm embrace
I always make such a fuss
Because I needed him
Needed him to love me enough for both of us

I never said
I never saw
That love was not enough

I was a broken boy

I was an abandoned soul

And I was
Addicted
To him

But, She
Entered my life

The Sphynx of the night
She was

A love I never knew
She was

An answer to my prayers
A force of life, where I had none
A calling in the dark
She was

She was like a crystal ball, seeing my future and my past
She was crystal clear, reflecting the best of me
She knew, life was more than just a sordid hourglass

And he became, and She became
One

A divine intervention,
A delight to my eyes
Uplifting, uprooting,
She, and he, looked so fine

And I was
Addicted
To the allure of Her life

How was I to know
It wasn't him
It wasn't me
That cut like a knife

That entered every fight
That gave us to the night
And abandoned us there
Oh no, She was near

In his every smile
In his every breath
In the love that he had
That became our death

Soon, I was Her's, and his, and them alone
There was no more longing, no sadness, nothing at all
Because I left it all
And let it fall
Like the dropping of a crystal ball
Shattering, violently, brilliantly, into a thousand pieces, strewn across the floor
And there was no more
Of me

I became Her
He became Her
Our glorious nights
Faded
Like worn out neon lights
Dissolving
Devolving
Into devilish lust
The redemption of flesh

And I became
A piece of meat
For him to consume
And to share
And what a dare to say he cared
This flesh was unwilling,
But the flesh is weak
And nightly, we'd revel in orgiastic delight
Seeing, but not seeing
The ruins around us
The wreck we'd become
The pleasure was too great
Too intense
To see ourselves in any other light
Any other light than the light of night

And when the beatings began, when the shame swallowed me, when the madness occurred, I was
Alone

The vixen had vanished
And, with Her, the fun
The delight must be saved for another night
The fun must be undone
For there is no pleasure without pain
No delight so bright that the black of night can't cover it's sight
Indeed
Days became hell
He held the pleasure of sin
I held no pleasure within
Beaten, scoured, used and abused
Was I

And gone
Was She
Until I found Her, one day
In the garden, waiting to play
She beckoned me closer
Invited me to tea
She promised me that She'd always be there
Always be near
For those times that I cared
That I dared
To break free of his bondage
To run away
To come closer to nothing
That something
Would wait for me there

A party, for me
A party, for three
Nevermind the pain
No longer was I alone
I found comfort in the garden
I found companionship in Her tea
I was found again, born again, a refugee delighting to be free

Funny, though,
As much as I was beaten
As much as I took flight
Under cloak of night
Going to the party that made it all right

Never, in the morning, did I find a trace in sight
Of my companions, of the pot of tea
Of the friendships I had made
Vanished with the rest of the night

But they were there, I swear
A comfort in the cold and dark
A refuge from his evil heart
Revelers in their own right
They took care of me, many a night

But She bewitched me
For She made me care
She made me love
The one who destroyed me
Him, who knew all my sins
And spat them back at me
I could not win

Into his rough arms I cried
Against his demands I gave in
Begging for love, kicked to the curb
There is no word for what I endured
And he loved me
In his own way
A master I could not betray
Beaten down, I could not believe
Believe in him, or God, or me
So
His love was, had to be, must be, enough for both of us
Because otherwise I couldn't make it through the night

And I was
Addicted
To love

To that sense of heartbreak, to that feeling of despair, to the hopelessness and
helplessness and knowing that no one cared
Yes, love
To wondering if I'd done all right
To wondering if I'd be beaten tonight
To hoping and praying and supplicating and humiliating and going on though the pain
never stops
Yes, love

I pledge allegiance
To Her

Because She can make it alright

I forgot, could not face the memories, of that garden of earthly delight
Of those pleasurable nights
Of a time when he and I didn't fight
But reveled in Her glorious light

No time to think, where did it all go?

My life, a blur
Just one hit, of Her
Takes the pain away
Takes the blame away
Makes memories disappear
Like shadows, flitting here and there
Where there is no air
Suffocating them
Suffocating me
Intoxifying me
Making it all clear..!
Then the curtains close

His love was enough for both of us
Her and I
His pain was enough to bear
With my blind eye

And I was
Addicted

No more joy, no more love, no more life
Just a hit
To make everything alright
For here comes the night
Let's play for a bit

Changes (all the time)
Jul 23, 2014

I strive to be something I'm not
Wait, is that true?
Do I strive?
Or can I even attain?
Or do I even want?
What is it that I'm not?

People always tell me, "you can change"
People love to lecture, "if only," "how could you," "don't you know better"
People love to sympathize, "I understand," "yes, life is rough," "make the best of what you've got"
But
People, all these faceless souls, yelling, crying, searching for answers
They don't really care
Cause those motherfuckers will never know

How can you picture a life on the City streets, strewn with garbage and human waste, covered with used needles and blood, picked at by cops on their beat...
How can you picture the will to go on in the face of tragedy, of starvation, of slowly dying and disappearing, everyone disgusted by me...
How can you picture the want and the need, the frailty of humanity, where bullets kill the innocent, where soup kitchens feed the weak...

You, with your suburban life, your pretty lawns, your Volvo on the street
You, with your high manners, your ladylike demeanor, your Prada shoes on your feet
You, with your fancy degrees, your charity at the social club, your slavishness to the latest beat

The words don't cross over
The feelings are untranslatable
Mere sign language with no interpreter around
Mere symbols without a Rosetta Stone to be found

Oh, and they try, reach out to the needy, as if a pat on the head, free lunch once a day, a wary smile on the streets, that these efforts will guide them to heaven
And what of me?
Well, I'm just a waypost, a check on the list, a duty considered done, a man of meager means whose soul they supposed to have saved
Stay away, you, just let me be

Yes, I'm an addict, yes, I'm a fucking whore, yes I'm a rebel, yes, just show me the fucking door
To the jails and prisons and institutions where they care for people like me
Reading their books round a circle,
Stating their names and disease,
Disowning themselves,
Til all that's left
Is a pile of bones where there once was a soul
"Victory!" they claim, another convert on their list, another waypost on the way to heaven

You know what? I'm fucking proud of who I am
It's a miracle I'm alive
But since I am, death can take his sweet ass time taking me away
I don't love it on the streets, no
But I have mad respect for those who live it
Those who fight every day towards no other goal than just living a day longer
Those who put up with abuse because deep down, they know they're better than that
Those who love life so much that being downtrodden, suffocated, scoured away... It's all in a day
That shines bright with the light of the sun,
That twinkles mischievously with the passage of stars,
That reminds them that Prada ain't what's real, that degrees don't count where it matters, that all the fancy talk of councilmen, lawyers, mayors and governors will never raise their lot in life
But the sun still shines bright when those Prada shoes break, the stars still twinkle while those politicians have one last drink

How funny it is, I used to be those "others." Who's to judge me as being an outsider when I can judge you just to same? Let's not judge.

Can I change? Can I give up the crack? Can I quit being a fucking whore? Can I strive to be something I'm not?
Hell no, I won't go
I can give up this life, but not to suit you, not so you can say that you converted one more today
Fuck you and your pretentious concern
Fuck you and your manicured lawns
Fuck you and your Volvo and your 3.5 kids and a dog
Crack is whack, but it's where I'm at
Meet me where I'm at, or don't even try
I strive
Every day
Every night
In every way

Not to be something I'm not,
But to be a fucking better version of what I've got

What's it that I'm not? An upstanding member of society? A law-abiding citizen? A man who likes women instead?
Who wants those things, those trappings, those symbols of suburban angst?
Deep down, you're terrified
I'm not
Cause I've been there, I've seen it, I faced it, I made it, and there ain't no thing I ain't ready for now
Too bad you clucked away all those years, marking your charts and penning your bills
I learned who I was and how to survive

There is no better version of me
So fuck y'all and your well intentioned smiles and prayers
I found God already
Right here inside myself

So next time you tell someone "you can change,"
Ask yourself, what are they changing into? Who are they changing for?
You know the answer
Let it be
I want to be the best version of me
And I know I can
I already am

(No) loss

Jul 24, 2014

I lost it all

Ono day, I woke up, and realized I couldn't go on
One day, my lover broke up with me
One day, I overdosed, lay comatose, sprawled on the bedroom floor
One day, I wish it all would end

I was a star
The envy of my peers
Yet

Something was missing
Something felt wrong, deep inside
Something went awry, somewhere, somehow
And I don't know what it was, and I don't know why

I never let on
No one ever knew
If I couldn't understand it, why should they?
That's my biggest regret today

And I had it all

The friends
The fun
The frolicking

The fates were on my side

So
Where did I go wrong?
How did I stumble, how did I fall
Into this abyss, so deep
Even I can't see the light of day?

It just happened, one day

My lover rescinded his love

And my heart broke

And I
Yes I
Unknowingly, ungratefully, unexpectedly
Went insane

My heart beating wildly inside my chest, I was gasping for air, screaming but no one could hear
Watching my world turn bleak, no, turn dark, turn empty, my vision failing, my pulse pumping
The ocean racing through my ears
And I was
Falling
Helplessly
I saw it happening, as if it were to another
Crumpled on the floor, spasmodic tempo in my muscles, convulsing back and forth
I knew
Then
That I couldn't survive, that I didn't want to survive, that without love there is no life, without him there was no me
In that second

I lost it all
The will to survive
The desire to see another day
The ability to move forward

And so I reached, excruciatingly, painfully, spasmodically, to the pills under the bed
Trembling, seizing, I unscrewed the fucking child proof caps (who decided I needed those?)
Counted out a few...
No, fuck it, I decided, somehow conscious enough, I'm not going to slowly slip away
I wanted my lover to see a grotesque image of a contorted body clamoring for air, swollen, spastic, eyes bulging out, shitting my pants, grabbing violently, puking blood...
I wanted him to feel my pain and know, deep inside, that he was the one that caused it all, that his act of betrayal had sealed my fate, that the blood I spewed was on his hands
So
I grabbed the full bottles
Dumped them down my throat
Gulping the poison
And I was happy, blissful, knowing death was near
There's something so good and right about seeing your end approach
I was playing God with my own life
Sealing my own destiny
Not afraid
No more questioning

And then
As I prepared myself to leave my body behind and enter a new world, as I was happy, for the first and last time I could ever remember, I lay convulsing but unaware, dying in this world, eager to fly to the next,
He came to me
And pulled it all away

I was destined to live

Fuck him, fuck my friends, fuck the establishment
Fuck me

I nearly had it all

And then I lost it all

I am God

Jul 29, 2014

I am master of my universe, Lord of all I see
With lifeblood pulsing through me
Giving life, inspiring breath into becoming flesh
And so flesh it shall remain

I alone hold the power
Life becomes death, darkness and decay
Oh, decadent souls, don't you know?
The devil is out to destroy you

Blood on my hands
Pierced into my palms
I stand, hanging, as if about to fall
Lost in motion, left behind
These unfeeling, all-seeing eyes, your time has come

To strike
To torture
To unrelentlessly destroy
Valiant, vain and victorious
Am I

These bastards, in my way
Conspiring to take me away
Hush hush is the word, as they quietly alight, into the night
There must be some sin about to begin

Drawing my sword against the coming evil
Mounting my steed in the light of dawn
Ready for battle against the sinners of this earth
They, who so content with their contempt, have set up a snare to enslave me
They are committing the ultimate sin

The blood is on my hands
Avenging my life
Creating their death
I have plowed forth, assailing, striking down, reaching out to these bitter, ignorant
hearts and crushing them in my fists, still beating, spewing warm blood, until,
screaming in agony, they expire

No man has power over my life
But I alone
I create my own destiny, I am master of my domain, Lord of my territories, keeper of the faith
For yes, I am faithful
That I alone have the power to create life, to cause death, and to protect myself against the vicissitudes of this earth, this universe, this pestilent existence
I alone may decide when it's over
I alone may decide when my time has come
Not this army of men who believe in false idols, this mass of humanity blindly following the teachings of the ages and aged, this torrent of persons so eager to turn, to topple, to overthrow, that which is their lifeblood
Oh if only they knew
My life is not theirs to destroy, my power is far too vast, my dominion too great
Mine alone is the power to create
And to vanquish
And to vanish
Into the glorious, shining light spewing forth, calling on the faithful (me)
To enter a new Kingdom
A new lordship
Calling on me to end this time on earth
To seize my power
And to dissolve into sweet clay and dust, holding firm to my power and destroying their blood-lust

I am my own Lord
I am my own personal Savior
I alone hold the power of life and death
And I choose..

From dust I became, to dust I shall return
On my terms
Faithful to myself, no power higher than I
I answer my own prayers and become
One
With the earth
I alone hold this power

For I am God of my existence

No day but today
Aug 3, 2014

No day but today.

To my true friends, comrades, brothers, addicts, fighting every day against prejudice, disease and "sin," let he who sins be the first to condemn...

A tear on my cheek for every life lost, a year destroyed by addiction, friends gone, lives taken...

To those staring addiction in the face, to those struggling against disease, to those living life on their own terms -

there is no day but today.

And I stand with you, weaker than you all, but stronger than you think. I know death, I know drugs, I know depression and despair. I know disease and destruction and the devil within. And I know damn well that I'm a survivor, despite all odds. Staring death, drugs and disease in the face, staring at my friends, alive and dead, staring at those who know and those who can't know, staring at sin and anarchy and the destruction of humanity, staring, especially, at me... I hope, for me, for you, for us, for them, that there is no future without a past, that there is no life without love, and that -

there is no day but today.

So much I've lost, so much I've gained, so much I've yet to discover..

I'm here, damn it all. I've chosen my life, my path, my friends, and I'm here to stay, and to say, thank you to those who have nourished me, those who have brought me back to life (though I hated you then), thank you to those I've taken care of, those who have taught me of angels and addicts, thank you to death for not taking me, thank you to life for bringing me back -

I'm here to discover, distinguish and deliver. I'm here to to be disowned, to be despised and to be destroyed. Fuck all that. I'm here because I deserve to be here. I'm here, because love and life need me and I need them, I'm here because, today -

there is no day but today.

And so I soldier on, knowing that each day brings renewal, that each life touched brings joy and happiness to me, to them, to the world. I won't fucking change for anyone. I love me, no matter where I'm at. Drugs and disease may be the death of me, but I'm not staring sadly into an unknown future, I'm not recounting past moments lost, I'm living now, in the present, in life, in sin, in the moment, in today.

There is no way but this way, no life that can't be lived, no joy that can't be shared, no sadness too strong, no disease too deep, no mountain too high, no valley too low -

There is no gay, no straight, no addict, no pure, no diseased, no clean, no right, no wrong, no good, no bad; these things all wash away. I am me. Take me as I as am. I need my candle. I need my smack. I need my life, back on track. I need you to not condemn but to love instead. I need to live each day as my last, each moment anew -

For there is no day but today.

Whispers
Aug 11, 2014

I'm standing, alone, in the middle of the street, surrounded by dead concrete
Watching life pass all around me
Watching the world go by me
Please, just let me be

I can't stand the noise anymore
People calling me a fucking whore
People showing me the door
As if their sins I would just ignore

Silence, please
Voices crashing in my head
I whimper, I hang my head
Throw myself onto the bed
Sometimes I think I'd be better off dead

Trying to quell the madness within
Trying to ignore my sin
Oh what a fate this is

Voices, voices
Screaming, crying, laughing, mocking, teasing
I listen to them
I know

I know my reality
Shadows flitting around, stealing my dignity
Because when I cry, and begin to die, there's some little lie that won't let me say
goodbye
Goodbye

To all the shadows with whom I converse
Goodbye
To the madness of this earth
What a curse!

I see so much
Where so little exists
I hear so much
Where people never visit

Surrounding me, confounding me, compounding my fears, mocking my tears
"Shut up!" I scream
But they don't listen, they don't hear, they don't care
They're not as real as they seem

Oh, I know this
But I forget

I fight to remember, when haunted by these spirits within
When fighting the devil, when engaging in sin
What a state I'm in

They're real, I swear
Again and again
But no one listens
No one cares
The shadows, they disappear,
Into the shroud of night,
Keeping the kingdom tight
Making my mind just right

Oh so wrong
I believe in them
I crash and burn for them
I cry, I try, I die, trying to fly
To quell the voices within
To run away, silence the din
To be myself, but I give in

I'm standing alone, surrounded by the cold concrete
But there's a pitter patter of feet on the streets
A whisper that screams, as if to beat
The coming storm, the abyss of heat

Swirling around, turning to the ground, supplicating my hands to the one who
understands

I hear you, though you're not there
Though you'll never care
And I will never dare
To be the one who has to bear
A lifetime of voices crystal clear
In my head, intensifying fear
Making me wish I wasn't here

I try to make them vanish

To disappear into the night
But instead they bring forth a light
To stay up til twilight
Penetrating, agonizing, suffering, they infiltrate my head
Oh I wish I was dead
Can't sleep the slumber of the weak
Can't carry the weight of all these people on the street
They're in my head
There's no other way
There's no light of day
There's no going back
To a past that won't last

I'm doomed to be tormented by voices
Though I made all the right choices
They chose me
And live in glee at my agony
Just let me be!

Whispers in the dark of night
Shadows that can't put up a fight
Encroaching me
Destroying me

Whispers, Whispers all around
Though no one is making a sound

Please
Just let me down

Rush

Aug 25, 2014

Feel the rush
Feel the blush, of happiness
Feel spun
Feel one, with nature, with your body, with your fellow man
Feel damned

Salvation lies, it would appear, in the bottom of a bottle of pills
Feel the chill
Fed to hell
But that salvation was not mine to have

Where do I turn for a savior?
Where is my god?

Flicker of flame, shadows in the dark
Rolling, bowling, watching shit arc
In the glass pipe, crystal clear
Smoking, slowly, now faster, now breathe, inhale, take in the rush
Don't let go til you're full
Let your mind wander, crazy, tripping
Tweaking
Poring over every detail, every line, every lie

My god, my salvation, is not in pills
It is in these rocks of glass, shattered, before me, ice, blue, chill
These are my poison pills

And when they go down, they go down easy
Feel the rush
Just a crush
That takes me to a whole new world, spinning, soaring, up above the clouds
So high
So fine
All that, is mine

Suck it in
This is my sin

But I'll take it, anyday, over that other life you promise, over that other God you worship, over those verses selling sin, not salvation
I'll take my chances, thanks

I'll take my baggie and my pipe
And the clouds surrounding me, embracing me, comforting me

Up high, there is no lie, everything is fine, and we go higher, and higher, reaching towards the sun, breathing deeply, exhaling and exalting at the bliss, oh what I wish, it all would stay forever

Keep me, I pray, in the clouds above
Feel the rush
Feel the happiness
Feel spun, at one, at peace, with yourself
This, you see, is my new love

No poison pills
Elixir of life instead
This time, better off in my head, than dead
And I sit, spinning, waiting for my rocket to come
With all this, be done
Rejoice in the sun
Where we all are becoming one

Grade A Ass
Aug 27, 2014

I prefer not to name the shame that was my game back in the day
You know, I know it, we all know it
Hooked on crack, ain't got nobody's back, but my own
Shot to hell, shit to sell, ass to grab, heart to stab
It's all in a day

Hey boy, who you calling ho?
You think you got more class than this ass?
Lemme see you try to run these streets for a day. Ok? Then we'll talk class

I be ho'ing it up all around town
I know, you know, we all think I'm a fucking clown
But out on my own, when the shit hits the fan, you live the life you're given, not some
fucking fairy tale
Fuck that
I got real problems
Where my shit at? Fucking ho
Steal off me, like a nigga, that's my shit boy, leave it alone
I be fighting for my right just to fight, let alone deal with these niggas stealing my shit
I ain't got the time
Sure as hell ain't gonna pay the fine
Cause when the time comes to call it a crime
I bounce, baby, bounce

This ass for sale, fifty percent off, buy one get the other cheek free, it's a steal of a deal
Cause you know what? I need that crack, ok? That shit you're selling ain't going for free,
man. I'd take it though. Just holla when you having a sale. Until then, one cheek in front
of the other one, sing it now, loud and proud

I ain't no baggie chaser
Baggie? Please
Let's talk hotel suites and Bentleys and fine moonshine
Baggie? Think I'm putting out for that? Oh girl you got some nerve, just cause your ass
ain't worth shit doesn't mean mine don't either. Oh no, clean that shit up before it rots
on your Juicy thong
Cause you got me wrong
I'm a ho, yeah, boy, I said it
An escort to the fucked up men paying to get their rocks off
Asserting my needs once I've got theirs by the balls
Cause they all fall
And shell out g's man, shell out for me
Oh because I'm good, real good, not your five and dime ho

No bitch, you get me and you get class ass, prime grade, what you don't think I'm worth it?

Worth ain't what's in your head, baby, aww, c'mon now kid, it's in your heart!

I just fucking with ya. Your worth is earned on the streets, and I don't see you doing no hustling, no grabbing, no stabbing

In fact, I think you think you're better than that

Hey nigga, ain't a one of us that could survive this world alone, so go on, dig your own hole

I get my crack right where I know it's at

I sell my ass right where the buyers at

I strip and moan to put on a fucking show, to these ugly, sordid douche bags thinking they're better than me because they hired my ass? Oh no, bitch, you only rented it, you couldn't afford full cost, you look cheap anyways, I'll pass

Once I score I run to the alley, high heels clacking, getting the needle out even before I sit my ass down

Injection

The pain of perfection

Doing it just right

Making life just right

For that moment, we niggas all in this together

Let your love shine baby! Shine

Cause daybreak, what's left is mine

Taken aside to make it through the day

Snorting lines off toilet seats, God I hope that bloods not mine. Crystal slamming into my mind, my mentality, shocking me back into existence, back into life

Slamming me

Belt around my arm, flex, yeah, this will just sting, oh mother fucker it's in I feel it it's burning pumping through me my dick is hard like you ain't never felt hard before

Yeah, that's the good shit

For that, I'll stay here all night

Cause I'm a classy ho

No hourly motels, no dirty sheets,

I escape in my Bentley to where my client waits

Cause that's the name of the damn game

Different client, different needs, different payments, but it's all the same. Enough to cover my drugs then you got we a deal, Shake on it. Or spit, like the motherfucker that you are.

I'ma one them nigs that made it
Ain't no shame
Take your shots in life
I shot further
So fuck off
Maybe some pussy will take your small shot, go on then, son, try

Who you calling ho? Oh honey, you've got a long way to go

Giving (up)
Aug 21, 2014

Sex is a rush, a rushing of parts and beings hurriedly, slowly now, passionately working their way to the final climax to create something beautiful and great.

Sex creates great.

That's not what I was taught
That's what made me slowly go insane
Sex is ok? But only for heterosexual. Only in the marriage bed. Only for the purpose of procreation. Nothing else is acceptable.

Sex is an act between two humans celebrating their love and affection for each other, to demonstrate the extent of their desire.

Sex brings us higher.

That's not what I was taught. I taught myself that love is bad, that sex is rape, that pain must follow.

I was taught to use drugs to numb the pain, to create an artificial sense of happiness and reality.

Those drugs only changed my perception, not reality. And when I broke through, I realized all I had done was be a dirty whore among these dirty sheets with no hope of salvation.

This life has broken you
Made false promises to you
Used fraud to induce you
But now, you have the power
And it is that hour
To seize back time
Rejoice in time
Make love in time

We are not eternal
Fraught with the kiss of death from the moment of birth
What a curse
But no, time, it bursts
Surrounding, confounding
Giving presence, giving essence
Making love worthwhile
Showing the start and course of our love, and where we shall stand

Salvation is our choice to choose, our life to have
Drugs be damned, I'm awake now
I'm alive
I never thought this would be me
Rejoicing in the light of day
But now I understand
And now I have overcome

I have been taught many things. What matters is what I lived and learned. That, alone, is the real reason for being, and the reason to press forward when all else seems so lost.

Never, never, never, give up.

Spun
Sep 1, 2014

Spun
And I'm done

I set my sights upon tomorrow
Where the world is less filled with sorrow
When the time comes that I no longer need to borrow

Cause I've borrowed hope, and fear, and money and drugs
Wish I had traded hugs
Cause there ain't no love
Between ho's and a hard place
Trust me, I've seen that face
Pockmarked, sallow and base
Crying for more, ain't none to have
Crying for peace, ain't none to find
You must be blind

I'm spun
Living the high life in the clouds above
Watching the world pass me by
Hey man, at least say hi!
Cause I see you ain't so fly
I've seen you when you cry
So hey, don't judge, don't hold a grudge
Don't hate
It's never too late

Pass me another
Hit
Yeah, that's it
Rolling, spinning, feeling good
It's all right in the hood
But when your mama comes calling
Don't be on the floor balling
She don't need to see her son like that
On crack
Out of whack
Scrambling for a sack
Trying to take back
Those good times, he once had
Now, it's all turned bad
And leaving him so sad

Inject me
Perfect me
In that moment, I alone
Know the world is so forlorn
Sitting with a needle in my arm
Hoping it'll be just the charm
To pull me back together
Cause there ain't no other
Nothing like crack to take you back to where it's at
The hood
Where the moonshine's always good
Where the cow jumps over the moon
And I heat up a spoon
Brown liquid bubbling up
Filling me up
So those times when I feel stuck
Lying in bed, lying in my head
I can remember the rush
Forget the pain
Just remember
The perfection of injection

Spun
And I'm done

City by the Bay
Sep 8, 2014

Put on my game face, say hello to another day
Plaster on a smile, say hey
To the man on the street, pissing his life away
Wait, that's me, I've fallen a long way
All I've got to say
Is
Just make it another day, in the City by the Bay

Cause I'm not ok, no
Forlorn and alone
Supplicate myself to the one who knows
Cause on the other side, the grass grows
Greener
So I've been told

Am I too old?

Life passed me by, a train in the dark
Fuck that, I live my life on a lark
On pins and needles, dodging dogs that bark
But the one thing hurting is my heart

Where is the kid I once was?
Covered in blood

What happened to my youth?
Taken away, in a coup
My darkness overtaking my life
Dooming me to nothing but a life of strife
Of bloodshed, of dying, yeah, that's right

I am greater than death, so it seems
To my body, I'm nothing but mean
Reflecting the world, reckless in greed
And bloodlust
Ravaging my soul, digging a hole
To throw my body in
Just another day on the dole

Death, please take me! I pray in suffering
But vengeful Death wants more suffering
Throwing myself on the floor, outside his door, supplicating
Please, end the suffering!

I've seen too much
Seen the secrets of death, and such
Is not meant to be known to mere mortals,
I've seen the darkness of holl
Right where I fell
Comatose, at the place I dwell

What can I say? It's just another fucking day
Plaster on my smile, say hey
To myself, on the streets, pissing my life away
No one left to inveigh for a better today
No one to care at all
So I fall
Drifting down to hell, I whisper the secrets that I'm not meant to tell

Sweet hell
Here I come
Riding the crystal fairy down the abyss
There's not a thing that I'll miss
Forgive me dear world,
But you've done this to me
Depression, drugs, now death
What's left?
Have you no pity, no sorrow, no fear or knowledge of what's best?
Condemn me while waltzing away to the door
That smile plastered on my face, covering up a sophisticated whore
Dance with me
Just once more

Suffering
Sep 11, 2014

Sitting here, by the side of my bed, all alone
Surrounded by people
Who don't care
Why am I the one always left out, always disregarded, always disrespected, always underappreciated?
Why am I the one thrown to the curb, knocked out, dragged down, by life?
Why am I alive?

I'm alone in a dark, dark world
Crying, every moment
Praying to be taken away
Praying to a God that doesn't exist
No one would lay this much suffering on a person, no one should have to persist
I'm broken, ok?
Battered
Abused
Forsaken
Ready to die

I'm ready
Heaven or hell or no afterlife at all
I don't give a shit
I just want this one done

So when the time comes
And I'm done
Who will remember? Who will give my eulogy? What is there to say?
Another life suffered, now it's over
Amen

Forsaken love
Sep 14, 2014

Say something
Anything, at all
I want to see your soul bare
I want you to go out on a limb, take a dare
I want to see that you care
Please, take me there

Cause I love you, I do
You love me too, don't you?
I don't see it in your actions
I don't see it in your eyes
Sometimes, though, I see it in your lies
Say something
Make me come alive

I'm staying here, should I move on?
Is your love, our lives, all gone?
What went wrong?

You gave me that crack
Now you can't take it back
We're stuck together, baby
Stuck for all time, maybe
Oh you make me crazy

And that's it, isn't that so?
That I'm crazy, and you gotta go
That I'm unzipped, and I can't sew
Who, who will hear my woes?
I'm dying, like a black rose
You're the only one that knows

Don't leave me
Take me back
Why do you hurt so good?
Did you take me cause you knew you could?
Not for love's sake
Love unforsaken
What wouldn't I give if I knew you would
Forsake me

I've given you my all
Here I stand, six feet tall
Trying to show you I've become so small
Without you, there is no Fall
No Spring, no seasons, nothing at all
Oh please, don't make me fall

I thought we had heaven
When we actually had hell
I thought love hurt
I think I've been cursed

I need you
Inflict that pain
I have nothing to lose, everything to gain
I won't run, I can't
I just want you to take me back

Say something
Anything at all
Show me you love me
Show me you care
Please, I'm begging you, take me there
My soul I've bared
My heart has cared
Show me you love me
Show me you care

Gone boy
Sep 23, 2014

Hello, are you there?
Cause I see in your eyes that you don't care
All I'm asking is that you treat me fair
Do you dare?

Because
I came to you in my hour of need
Looking, longing for a love between
I had to have you, don't you see?
Abandoned, I threw myself at your mercy, made it your choice to take me or leave me
But I couldn't just let myself be
There was no choice, no other way
I needed you that day

But - I see this now - there was something you needed too
There was something that you needed me to do
You needed a warm body by your side
You needed a person to put yourself inside
You needed to own me, even if I would die
Even better if you could make me cry
You knew I wasn't strong enough to say goodbye

So when I asked for your love, you said yes
Let me guess
Was it because you knew all along? Did you need to make yourself feel strong?
What was it that you felt, in those days long gone?
What did you want from me, to sing you a fucking lullaby song?
Or just be a body that you could piss on

My beating heart I gave to you
My body I gave up for you
But you cursed it all
You saw me as nothing but a rag doll, while I was curled up into a ball, for you to give
your all, please just let me fall, so I can heed the call, break down the wall, walk that
long hall to heaven, or am I now doomed to hell?
My loving heart, you mangled
My virgin soul, you strangled
I felt betrayed, my innocence destroyed
Because while I lay there crying, lay there dying, you were with some other boy
To you I was nothing but a toy, molded by your hands into a puppet with which you
could play
That was my bleeding heart you mangled that day

This toy is a real boy, but you'll never care, you'll never dare, to see me as a man, as an equal, oh that's rich
You just see me as your bitch
You'd rather see me dead, hitched to a hearse that drags me into a ditch

I've cried all my tears
You've ruined so many years
Never to be lived again
Why did you beat me?
Why did you need me?
You needed a priest, to confess all your sins
All that evil you held within
Even an exorcism couldn't rob you of the devil you possessed
You were a monster, to me and all the rest
So many souls wounded, scattered to the dark, far corners of the earth, not that it matters
No one left to show them mercy
No one left to show them love
Like me, the only solace can come from above
Where there is no God
The battle between good and evil is done, so it was said
It must have been, because you left me for dead
All those nights that I shared your bed
All for naught, just when I thought that we would be wed
Oh you played vicious games with my head

I was such a fool, late to come around
You let me down
In a high stakes game of risk
All you wanted was my dick
But I gave to you my all
My mind, my soul, my body, those things you treated like a doll
Barren, battered and abused
Because of you I was completely subdued

And I was dead inside
You lacked the decency to even bury me alive, wide eyed, watching the world pass me by
I was dying, didn't you see?
You fucked with my head, kept me chained to that bed
Words of contempt were all I was fed
I loved you, but I couldn't get through to you
I was a stranger to you
You, who fucked around with so many men
You, who beat me nightly, calling me the whore
Oh, no more

I gave you my all
I've paid my damn fee
Juct let me be

I wasn't the whore you said I was
No it was you who was the whore, renting me out like a pimp does
To the girls he sees as flesh, not human, just a name upon which he could claim his
fame (and his fee)
As long as the clients came
As long as his girls came (oh honey, they could play that game)
He would mark his name
On each breast, sealing his ownership
Of those pieces of filth upon which he exists
Worse than him, though, you weren't content until I was writhing in pain
Suffering the agony of the cross in silence, my body being maimed
Fuck you, oh so righteous
Putting me in my place
Throwing salt on my wounds and in my face
Cutting me open, just to see my blood
Just to enjoy that agony, just to release those black doves
To know that you made me, you saved me, you loved me, you cursed me
Oh couldn't you see?
I just wanted to live a life that was ours
Carefree, having fun, making love under the moon and the light of the stars

I let you fuck me anytime
Because I thought you were mine
I didn't know you had so many others
I didn't know you'd whore me out, just like you did your mother
All the times that I felt pain
All the blood and tears shed in my name
All the times I cried out for help, just a little whelp
Suffering
Suffocating
You said I'd be fine
You used me like a whore at a five-and-dime
But, oh God, even if I could take back time, I'd still make you mine, I'd still like to dine,
enjoy fine wine, pretend that our love still exists, just for a bit

But now I'm not fine, no, I'm not
But fuck it, I'm all that I've got
I know you don't care whether I make it or not
But I survived without you, so go to hell
I clawed my way out from under your spell
My dignity had long ago died
But my spirit always survived

I knew I could, and I knew I would, escape you somehow, someday, some way
Your brutal fists, even in the light of day
Your cruel words, tossed out like you were pitching hay
What were you thinking
All those times that we fought?
What were you doing with that flesh that you got?
But you couldn't put out the fire in my heart, it burns red hot
Burning me, burning you, burning the mirage of an image that we're not
We're not a model couple, God help me if we are
You're nothing but a drunk, stumbling home from the bar
This time, you've gone too far

How could love be so cruel?, I want to know
How come black ravens ravished the garden where red roses were supposed to grow?
You never wanted me, no, you needed me
Like a sock puppet you could play with at will
Like a whore you could abuse without regret, never paying the bill
You became a monster, not the man that I met
Back in the day, when our lives were gay, and I had my heart set

And so I gave myself
And now I'm running to save myself
Life goes on, they say, even when you're gone
Oh I hope you're gone
There's room in that ditch for you too
Now you know what it's like to kill yourself, don't you
I hope you enjoy being six feet under, I'm not jealous of the view
See you in the life hereafter, my boo

So I will go on
And I will be strong
I don't know if life is worth living
But I wasn't going to die for you
I'll find out for myself what life is all about, of that I have no doubt
I'll think of you, but I won't pray for you
In my heart, you're already gone

Lie

Oct 20, 2014

I'm not an addict, no, that's a lie
But hey, sometimes I like to get high, get what's mine, get a piece of the pie
Cause the world's a rough place sometimes, it's do or die
Don't be judgmental, you're nothing to me
No one that I need, to watch me pee in a cup, end up in the dump
I'm no chump

I just like to get high

But I know my limits, yeah, I know when it's enough
It's just that, some days are so rough
And I wonder, am I tough enough?
I don't know, so I lay low
Crack pipe in hand, just trying to score some blow
Slam a needle in my arm, I'm sure there's no harm
Life sure ain't like this back home at the farm

Here its nothing but concrete and glass
And cigarette butts
Hey sir, can I have a light? I'm not trying to start a fight, just hoping for hope that is not
quite there
When I lay down to sleep, on the street, like a pile of meat, I'm greeted by the local
cops, just trying to get one off
Fuck the establishment
I just wanted to establish it
Oh, and get one more hit

I'm not an addict, no, that's a lie
But don't judge me for trying to get high
You see me on the streets, don't say hi or bye
Just see a piece of filth, a man in the gutter, slamming himself senseless so he can
make sense of it
That's right, you don't know the half of it
I've got my pipe to make the world right, I've got my blow to keep in tow
I've got my dope, like a Pope on a rope, strapped to my side

I know where I come from, I know where I'm headed
But I don't know where I'm at
Chasing down alley cats who dare holler at me! Just let me be
I ain't no criminal, though I might be insane
Oh the fun had in honor of my name
Know what? I'm fucking tough enough, yeah, I am

But I don't give a damn
I like to live life on the lam
Living the concrete life on the concrete streets
It don't matter where I'm at
Do you doubt that?

I'm still figuring out who I am. I'm still searching for someone that gives a damn.

But I know I'm not alone, and neither are you. Life is full of surprises, full of unknowns, full of hope and regret. I've made it this far, I know you can too. If you stay strong, you can live on. Choose life, not strife. Choose hope, not dope. Choose yourself, don't live for someone else. Above all, choose love. Love yourself first. I believe in you.

Made in the USA
Columbia, SC
21 March 2023